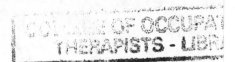

What's all this about Stress

RC OT Royal College of
Occupational
Therapists

WITHDRAWN

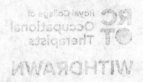

What's all this about Stress

Brenda Davison

TUDOR

© B. Davison 1999

First published in Great Britain by Tudor Business Publishing Limited.

A CIP catalogue for this book is available from the British Library

ISBN 1 872807 33 X

The right of Brenda Davison to be identified as the author
of this work has been asserted by her in accordance with the
Copyright, Designs and Patents Act 1988.

Typeset by Bitter & Twisted, N. Wales

Printed and bound by Athenaeum Press, Ltd.,
Gateshead, Tyne & Wear.

I dedicate this book to the memory of my father,
John Thompson,
whose invisible presence in my life,
since his untimely death whilst I was still in my 'teens,
has been the spur to my achievement.

About the author

Brenda Davison is a self-employed training and development consultant who specialises in personal and professional development. She has a wide clientele and is well-known for her expertise in stress management as well as for her light-hearted and interactive presentation style.

Brenda admits to her own share of life's traumas but has always been a fighter. "The tougher the challenge, the greater was my determination", she says. "Although life was often difficult, and sometimes very painful, I made it through to where I am today, and my greatest desire is to share with others who are struggling along the way some of the things that I have learned, to encourage them, and to help make their pathway a little easier."

Brenda set up her own consultancy in 1992 after a long career in the National Health Service, latterly in training and development at Aintree Hospitals, Liverpool. She changed careers moving into training in 1989 after gaining a Masters Degree at Salford University. Health Service re-organisation had caused her to re-appraise her professional direction after more than 25 years working as an occupational therapist, for the last ten of those years in a management role. She has also lectured at the Liverpool Business School where amongst other things she taught management and self-development skills.

She is married, for the second time, to John who is now retired and helps her in her work. They live in Bebington on the Wirral, and spend more and more of their time sailing, most recently in the Menai Straits, but with big plans to head for the Mediterranean. However, Brenda assures us that she has no plans to retire, and in fact is starting another career as a writer to complement her training and lecturing.

Acknowledgements

My grateful thanks go to all of my friends, family and colleagues who have helped with the preparation of this book.

To John, my husband, my inspiration and my support, who has prepared the diagrams, and painstakingly checked my manuscript.

To Carolyn, my daughter, whose encouragement and objective appraisal have been so valuable, together with her advice on alternative therapies and assistance with research.

To Kathryne Russell, my valued colleague, for her assistance in checking the factual content and making suggestions for improvement.

To former colleagues at the Liverpool John Moores University for their encouragement.

To my friends at Lancashire Ambulance Service and in Lancashire Education Department, together with the many others who have attended my courses, for their feedback on the material and how they have used it for themselves.

Brenda Davison

Contents

Introduction

List of diagrams

Diagram

Factfiles

Introduction

It seems to have become fashionable to talk about stress. There are numerous articles in magazines and business journals warning of its dangers. We see adverts for seminars in its management. It is common to hear the phrase, "I'm stressed out!" and we are told that the country is losing 360 million working days because of illness each year, at least half of which is stress-related and which is estimated to be costing UK industry something in the region of £4 billion.

On the other hand there are still those who deny its existence. They say, "My grandmother survived two world wars, was bombed out of her home, raised seven children and buried two others, yet lived to be ninety and had no idea that there was such a thing as stress." They imply, or even openly state, that stress is a sign of weakness, it is "all in the mind", and all we need to do is "pull ourselves together".

What is the reality, then? Is there more of it around today than in our grandparents' day, or are we just being weak and feeble when we should be being stoical and brave? Is there really more stress around in the comparatively prosperous, more peaceful, late 20th century than in the war years?

I have written this book to share with you, the reader, an overview of current teaching and thinking on stress. I have drawn upon my experience as a stress management consultant and trainer, which spans over 20 years. During that time I have worked with ordinary men and women from all walks of life and share with you in this book some of the things that they have found helpful, and some of the things they have taught me. In each chapter you will find stories of these real people, illustrating their problems and how stress has affected them.

In some situations I have also described how they tackled their stress-related problems In others I have left you, the reader, to work out, guided by the information in the chapter, how you think that person should tackle them. Some of the illustrations are drawn from my own life. Being a stress management consultant does not guarantee immunity from stress, but does increase range of options for coping.

There are many reasons why people attend stress management seminars, seek individual help, or read books on the subject. I wonder what has drawn you to this particular book? What is it that you want to know? Perhaps you have a problem and wonder whether it is caused by stress. Maybe your GP has told you that something you have consulted him/her about is "stress related". Are you wondering whether perhaps you are stressed? Or are you just under pressure? Maybe you are just over-worked? Perhaps you are aware that your work or your relationships are being affected by your feelings of excessive pressure.

If you think you might be stressed, it is possible that you are feeling guilty about it, telling yourself that you should be able to cope more effectively. It may be that you feel you ought not to admit to it, particularly at work, because you fear that you will never get promoted if you do, or you believe that it is a sign of weakness. It may be that you think of it as something only executives and people in high-powered jobs suffer from.

It could be that you are reading this book in order to help someone else, a family member or colleague perhaps. If you are a manager you need to understand the effects of stress on your staff. You need to be able to understand how it can affect work performance, and what the signs are that might help you detect it in your staff. An appreciation of environmental causes of stress as well as organisational causes will help you prevent its detrimental effects. You need to have a concern for your responsibilities as a manager in this area, not only to avoid possible litigation and be seen to comply with health and safety policy, but to improve work performance and guide your staff through stressful times, helping them grow and develop. Excessive stress affects how well we do our job, causes mistakes and accidents, and affects our relationships and our emotional health. So the bottom line is that it will affect productivity.

Whatever the reason, this book has been written to help you, the reader, understand just what stress is and why some people seem to be affected by it more than others. It will help you to appreciate your own stress levels, and enable you to recognise it in colleagues or family members. You will also learn what you can do to handle it more effectively and how to become more stress-proof.

My aim in writing this book has been to share with a wider audience the subject of my stress seminars. I trust you will find what you are looking for in its pages, and if only one person's life is changed as a result of reading it then the effort will have been worth while. As Ralph Waldo Emerson said, "To leave the world a bit better .....to know even one life has breathed easier because you have lived. This is to have succeeded". I hope that person will be you.

All of the people mentioned in this book are real people but their names and details have been changed in order to protect their anonymity.

chapter one

All in the mind

Since the 1980s the word stress has increasingly become part of our modern vocabulary. The term is often used quite casually when the ability to cope with day-to-day problems has reached crisis point. But it is not a new phenomenon. What is new is the recognition of its damaging, longer-term physiological and psychological effects. These effects were not recognised in our grandparents' day. Stress took its toll then as it does now, but there was not the awareness that the cause was stress. Doctors were not as skilled in diagnosing stress related-illness, even if their patients consulted them. Remember, there was no National Health Service then.

Stress is not the same as ill-health, but it can have serious outcomes. It can result in both physical and mental illness when the pressures are high and continue for some time. The effects of stress can last for a long period of time and can be very damaging.

Simon

As he closed and locked his car door Simon sighed and picked up his briefcase before scanning the high street for number 23. He was parked on double yellows again, but really he did not have the time to walk from the car park in the next block. This would be his third call this morning and Simon was hoping for greater success than he had had so far, but time was the enemy. As a photocopier salesman his task this morning was to interest this company in the latest all singing, all dancing model. As newly-promoted sales manager at 27 years of age, there was a lot of pressure on him to set an example through his level of business and justify the company's faith in him.

With the new job he had taken on staff management as well as the responsibility of managing the sales department. There were associated marketing tasks, and set targets to increase the level of business. He was pleased at his promotion but felt that the reasons for it were probably as much economic as anything else. The previous manager had retired early and after a lifetime with the same company had been receiving a salary vastly in excess of the one that Simon was now receiving. Simon was glad of the increase in his salary, and he and his fiancée, Beth, had been able to put their names down for a house on a new estate. He had to discuss the strategy for a proposed exhibition with the rest of his team. He found this hard because he had never managed staff before and there was one person who always gave him a hard time, Maudsley. Maudsley was 35, had been with the company three months longer than Simon, and had thought himself in line for the sales manager's job. He hadn't got it and now he was challenging Simon at every turn. He would criticise Simon's suggestions and, even when the rest of the team agreed, Maudsley would find some reason to back out and not be involved. Simon suspected that he was sowing discontent and sabotage behind his back.

Simon wished he had more energy to bring to the job but the harder he worked the more of a mess of things he seemed to make. He would wake in the mornings heavy-eyed, with an incipient headache, which usually asserted its presence before he had left the house. Then he'd forget where he'd put things, his car keys for example, and even important pieces of paper such as his sales figures which he had to input onto the computer. Last week he even forgot Beth's birthday and was only saved by the fact that he'd bought her present several week's earlier and was able to produce it when he suddenly remembered the date. He usually rushed off to work without breakfast, and instead of being excited by the challenge of his new job he was dreading every day.

It didn't help that the sales team was one person down since one member had gone off on sick leave, and had been off for six weeks now. His sick note had said "stress". Simon found it difficult to sympathise with this. It was his belief that stress was something only executives suffered from, not 26-year-old salesmen. He believed that when your GP said that you were suffering from stress he really meant that you were imagining it and there was no substance for your ailments. This belief was reinforced by the fact that he himself had been to see his GP only last week, nagged by Beth, because of all the headaches he'd been getting. The result was just as he'd suspected. "Stress", his GP had said. "Rubbish", thought Simon, "a young man like me doesn't get stress. Stress is all in the mind, and it means that you are weak and can't cope. I don't suffer from stress. Look at me, only 27 years old and already they've made me sales manager. Where would I be if I gave in to stress? They gave me this job because I can cope. I exceeded my sales targets by 5% last month and I'm on my way to doing the same this month. I should get some of my figures done before I have to make that presentation at three o'clock and if I can persuade the cheeky young madam in admin. to do my photocopying for me I might even be able to get round to Beth's before seven. I'm no weakling suffering from stress."

There are a lot of people who, like Simon, see stress as a sign of weakness and therefore ignore signs of it in themselves. They believe that you should not admit to stress, but somehow "pull your socks up" and get on with it. They see stress as a mental condition. The stigma attached to admitting to stress still exists.

Simon needs to understand the mechanism of stress and how physical, and mental, symptoms could be caused by stress: it is a very real phenomenon with a physical basis as well as mental. His definition of stress, as we saw, was that it was all in the mind, and something that weaklings suffered from, not healthy young men.

What is the definition of stress? I recently came across a definition which describes it as "the degree of tension, anxiety and/or pressure experienced by you". I like this definition because it emphasises the fact that stress is your unique experience. Someone else may have a different amount of tension in a similar situation.

There is also the definition used by the Health and Safety Executive: "The reaction people have to excessive pressures or other types of demand placed on them. It arises when they worry that they can't cope." This indicates that when we interpret a situation as being stressful we further increase our stress by worrying about it.

The word stress itself has been used for centuries and comes from the Latin word *stringere* meaning to draw tight. A French physiologist named Bernard[1] recognised the importance of balance in an organic system, and that this balance can be disrupted by environmental change. Hans Selye[2], an American physiologist writing in the 1920s, used the word stress to mean a collapse of this balance. He was the first to use the term in connection with human beings and was referring to the general breakdown of an individual's organic system in response to the wear and tear of modern life. When our balance (our equilibrium) is disturbed by excessive pressure, by imposed change, by shock, etc. our body uses up massive amounts of adaptation energy trying to restore the balance. Each one of us has only so much of this energy and when we run out of it stress results. But it is not just the individual's reactions and perceptions which determine the degree of stress. The nature of the work done and individual circumstances play a large part.

In 1995, some research was done on work-related stress for the Health and Safety Executive, and this was updated in 1997. The author[3] attempted to identify which were the most stressful jobs in Britain at that time. These were found to be the prison service, uniformed services, police, fire and ambulance, social work, doctors, dentists and nurses, and teachers. The next group included mining, armed forces, construction, management, acting, journalism, linguistics, film production, professional sport, catering and hotel work, and public transport.

Experienced stress researchers independently evaluated each of these jobs on a 10 point scale, from least stressful (1) to most stressful (10). All the above jobs scored more than 6.5 (very stressful) and the first group all scored more than 7.7 (extremely stressful). In updating the research, it was found that almost every job in Britain at that time was more stressful than it had been a decade previously and the stress levels associated with many of them were reported to be disturbingly high.

It may not at first be obvious what these jobs have in common which causes stress. There are some factors that are individual to those jobs, but there is one factor which they all have in common and that is change. All of these jobs have been subject to enormous changes in the last decade alone.

We are living in an age of unprecedented change. The saying is that "Change is the only constant in today's world", and you can see this if you look back over the changes that have taken place during your lifetime, no matter how old you are. We take the motor car and the aeroplane very much for granted today and yet there are people still alive who remember an age when horse-drawn transport was the norm.

A generation ago changes to technology, affecting the way people did their jobs, might occur maybe twice in a 30 year career. Now those types of changes take place every five years or so, and are getting faster. We have to be constantly in a learning mode, always trying to keep up. You order a new computer and it has been superseded by a faster model with more features almost before it has been delivered.

Companies are affected by change: many of these are the result of global changes, changes in markets, customer expectations, economic upturns and downswings, which mean that they have to be not only ready to move with the times, but actively anticipating trends so that they can stay ahead of the competition and keep their business viable. They have to diversify, specialise, outsource, downsize, and upsize (or as the Americans euphemistically say right-size). As a result of this they have to be very flexible and responsive, and to do this they need a flexible workforce. This means being flexible in mental attitudes and in willingness to adopt new working practices, new technology, scientific advances, etc. It also means being flexible in the sense that they are making more use of contracted workers, part-timers, shift workers, consultants and free-lance workers, temporary staff, and staff on non-standard contracts.

In a recent book, *Jobshift,* the author, William Bridges[4], says that the concept of the traditional job is becoming a historical artefact, and that only 57% of Britain's workforce now remains in traditional employment. The result of this is that the jobs-for-life security once enjoyed by workers, professionals and managers has disappeared, replaced with the threat of downsizing and the obsession with deadlines and performance reviews, which have extended deep into the public as well as the private sectors.

The communications tools of modern life - fax machines, pagers, mobile phones - are exacerbating the pressures. It is less easy to get away from work, or to be "unavailable" for short periods. All of this is making enormous demands upon individuals' adaptation energy and increasing the likelihood of excessive stress and its related problems.

Alongside this we become aware of a vacuum created by the rapid breakdown of structures of intimacy and support, such as the extended family, along with the weakening of traditional hierarchies, rituals and religious beliefs. These supports in days gone by played an enormous part in helping people withstand excessive and unhealthy stress. In fact researchers who have studied the Italian-Americans of Roseto, Pennsylvania, USA[5], came to the conclusion that the extended family and community, with its high level of connectedness in the first generation of immigrants, protected them from the ill effects of their traditional high-fat diets and high levels of smoking. This protection has been lost by the second generation who live in typical nuclear families with all of the social isolation characteristics of modern life. They now experience the same incidence of coronary heart disease as other Americans, whilst the previous generation had a lower-than-expected incidence.

There are widespread changes affecting the framework of family life everywhere.

Nowadays it is common for both partners of a couple to be working, whether or not there are children. Did you notice my use of the word partner? Marriage appears no longer to be the central unit at the core of our society. The social stigma of illegitimate children and living together has gone. A huge number of parents are single parents with no partner to give emotional or economic support. Gays and lesbians are struggling for recognition and removal of prejudice, to mention but a few of the changes which are happening in our society.

Then there is environmental stress which can be caused, for example, by cramped, inadequate housing, violence, noise, crowding, dirt and pollution. We read about sick-building syndrome allegedly caused by lack of natural light and fresh-air, as well as static electricity, pollution, noise, and numerous other factors within the design and layout of many working environments.

Stress has always been with us. But it, and its effects, are more readily recognised today, and the pace and change of modern life has turned stress into a growing epidemic. No-one is immune - stress is found on the factory floor, in the secretarial pool, in the IT suite, at the kitchen sink, on the football pitch, in the elderly and in the young, as well as in the boardroom.

It is becoming an industrial injury said to be outstripping the more traditional causes of sickness absence which were known to the older generation, such as black lung, white finger, and chicken plucker's arm. It is even replacing backache as a reason for absence. However stress is not an illness in itself; it is a life problem. Everyone is vulnerable: when pressure piles up, control is lost and our coping abilities break down. It is then that we experience stress. Rapid change disturbs our comfort zone and challenges our coping mechanisms. Our personality is often a decisive factor in how we react. We find ourselves being turned on and challenged, or brought down by our circumstances. But stress is not all bad. Stress is an important motivator.

The problem that Simon was facing after his promotion was that the extra hours and increased pressure were making him very tired. Some nights he stayed until after nine and was so exhausted afterwards he'd go straight back to his mother's and fall into bed. Even then he would have difficulties sleeping as his mind kept on turning over and over again the events of the day, and worrying about the things he had to do the next day. This was particularly bad whenever he had to face a new challenge like the exhibition stand he had to design, or the presentation about the exhibition which he was due to make to the management board. Presentations were to him an exquisite form of torture to be got through somehow. There were times when he thought he'd rather face a mad bull than give a presentation. The sweaty palms, wobbly knees, nervous stomach and throbbing headache were all a familiar part of it by now, and it didn't seem to be getting much easier with practice.

We need some stress to help us remain active and energised. Boredom can be as stressful as burnout. Stress keeps us stimulated and is reported to help prolong active live. Without stress we would achieve nothing and be like an unused engine, suffering from rustout. In parts of Russia there are 40 to 60 people per 100,000 of the population, who are over 100 years old[6]. One common link in all societies where this is a phenomenon is thought to be that their elderly continue to work, playing an active part in the business of their community, both physically and mentally, until the day they die. Lifespans are found to be shortened in groups that generally do not appear to have much control over their stress: in the fire service, in air traffic controllers, in police, and in assembly line workers.

Stress has always been with us, but it and its damaging effects are more easily recognised today, and the fast pace of change is responsible for an increased incidence of stress. But stress can be valuable, even necessary, to help us succeed in life. In subsequent chapters I shall explain in more detail how stress affects the human body, how its effects can be minimised and how you can prevent good stress from becoming bad stress and having a negative effect on mental and physical health. In understanding this process you can take steps to promote good stress-management practice for yourself, your family and your work colleagues, which will lead to a healthier and more energised lifestyle, and an extended lifespan.

References

1. Michell and Larson, quoted in "Behaviour in Organisations Unit 5: Stress and its Management", Liverpool John Moores University teaching material.

2. Selye, Hans (1950) *Stress*, Montreal, Octa.

3. University of Manchester Institute of Science and Technology, (1987) "Understanding Stress", HMSO.

4. Bridges, William (1995) *Jobshift: How to Prosper in a Workplace Without Jobs,* Nicholas Brealey.

5. Weil, Andrew, (1995) *Spontaneous Healing*, Warner Books, London.

6. Hanson, Dr. Peter (1986) *The Joy of Stress*, Cox and Wyman, Reading.

chapter two

The straw that breaks the camel's back

The difference between stress and pressure, or between being stressed and just having too much to do, is not always easy to define. One of the ways in which the difference can be measured is: "Would an added responsibility at work, or increased pressure at home, increase or decrease my efficiency?"

Claire

The familiar rattle of chairs being placed on tables sounded from the classroom next door. Claire hastily began to gather up her papers and stuff them into an already overcrowded briefcase. She had been trying desperately to catch up on the ever-present paperwork which teachers need to complete, using the few precious moments at the end of the day when the pupils had gone home and silence reigned. She valued these few moments at the end of the day, but they were never long enough.

Now the caretaker was approaching and in a moment the familiar face of Fred, who had been with the school longer than any of the present staff could remember, would be here to attack the debris left by 3G at the end of another school day. Not that Fred would deliberately prevent her from carrying on with her work, but he'd be chatty, and want to discuss the latest football results as he worked. As he steadily worked his way towards her desk Claire would receive the unspoken message loud and clear, "Time to pack up now, because I want to get finished and go home."

Claire had tried taking her work into the staff room, but it took twice if not three times as long in there. She would inevitably be drawn into some argument about the respective merits of the Boat Museum over the Mining Museum for Key Stage 3 project work. If only she could find a quiet place to get on with all that she needed to do: marking, lesson preparation, adding up the dinner money, collating statistics and so on. She'd even wondered whether she could take her work into the stock room, but the fear of getting locked in at the end of the day prevented her.

She was supposed to have a "free period" (non-contact time was what they called it these days) at least once a week. But inevitably she had to give this up to cover for colleagues who were absent due to sickness, or who had gone off on a training course. Usually it was sickness, they were all so busy these days. The hectic pace of teaching coupled with all the preparation and paperwork took its toll, and as term advanced more and more teachers went down with flu, bronchitis, tummy bugs, or just plain stress.

"I am not stressed though," thought Claire, "only wimps get stressed. I can cope. I enjoy my job. I just have too much to do". If only the government would lay off making changes to the education system for a bit I might be able to catch up. She suspected that they never would.

She knew that the pattern this evening would be much the same as last night, and the night before. She would get home about five, collecting the children from her mother's as she went. She would prepare tea and feed them all. Then wash up, and put some washing in the machine whilst listening to all the events in her children's day. Later, when they were in bed, she would slump in front of the TV feeling guilty about all the work she had brought home and attempting to gather the energy to get down to it. She would then probably fall asleep and wake at eight when Peter came home from work. Having put his tea in front of him, and chatted with him whilst he ate, she would then settle herself down at the kitchen table with her marking and lesson preparation until she could do no more. Usually about ten-thirty she would join Peter for a bedtime drink before falling into bed, exhausted and often sleepless. There had to be more to life than this, hadn't there? If they tried to make love she found herself still thinking about work and the class she would be teaching the next day so the process would be a mechanical one, rather than spontaneous and loving. "I do not think I am stressed, I am just over-worked and under pressure but I am not sure I know the difference".

Claire was finding herself over-worked and under pressure. To help her and others who may be asking a similar question it would be useful to look at the Human Function Curve, and ask, "Would added pressure take you so far up the curve that your performance started to decline instead of improve?"

Diagram 1

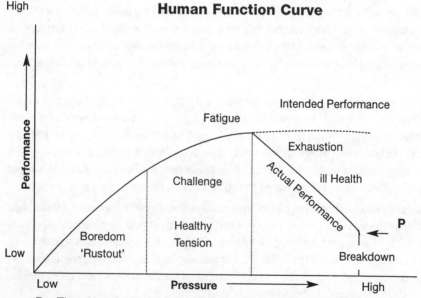

Human Function Curve

P = The point at which minimal pressure may bring on a breakdown

Based on The Human Function Curve, Dr. Peter Nixon 1987[1]

The Human Function Curve demonstrates that the need for increased performance is equalled by an appropriate degree of pressure from within ourselves. The result is sufficient stress to cause a state of healthy tension in which we do well. Stress is needed to help us function well in life. Too little and we are laid back to the extent that we are in the rustout zone. Too much and we are heading for exhaustion and possible serious illness, because there is a point on this curve at which the smallest added pressure can trigger physical or mental breakdown. What we really need is just enough to keep us on our toes and in a state of healthy tension, somewhere in the middle of the graph.

Good stress motivates you to achieve success, and is the driving force in most of our lives. It is also the salt and spice of life and to have no stress we would have to be dead. It makes life interesting and enjoyable and motivates us. In fact people often create stress for themselves, setting themselves deadlines and targets to meet, putting themselves under pressure to increase the stress response, in order to get themselves to work more effectively.

The more challenging or difficult the situation, the more stress or pressure we need. The pressure helps us to give of our best. When things get too much we may occasionally long for the solitude of a desert island where nothing ever happens, but we would soon get bored with not having enough to do and might begin to suffer from rustout which can be as stressful as burnout.

So stress is not all bad, but pressure can become unhealthy stress or dis-stress when there is too much of it, when it continues unchecked, or when our perceptions of it are that we can not cope.

When our anxiety to do well in a situation increases the degree of nervous or physical stimulation to the point where we are overstressed, instead of performing well, we do very badly. Take job interviews for example. For some people these can be quite nerve racking. You may get so worried about it that your very nervousness prevents you from doing your best and you end up making a mess of it, tripping over words, forgetting what you were going to say, going red in the face, and trying to control sweaty palms and trembling knees, instead of calmly and confidently convincing the interviewers that you are the person for the job. Does that sound familiar? In other words pressure is a driving and positive force until it exceeds your ability to cope, after which time your emotional or physical or behavioural system can break down. This is when pressure has turned to stress.

As you will see from the definitions in Chapter One, stress is considered to be an internal state or reaction to anything we consciously or unconsciously perceive as a challenge or a threat, either real or imagined. When we perceive something to be stressful it can evoke feelings of frustration, fear, conflict, pressure, hurt, anger, sadness, inadequacy, guilt, loneliness, or confusion. Individuals feel stressed when they are sacked, or when they lose a loved one (negative stress) as well as when they are promoted, or get married (positive stress).

*Going to the dentist is another situation which could illustrate this point. For a large part of the population, going to the dentist is "one of those things". We do not particularly enjoy it but in order to be free of pain, or to have teeth which look good, we put up with it, make our appointments and go. Other people become so anxious when there is a need to go to the dentist that they simply cannot do it. I have met people who have made the appointment and, even though they were in acute pain, turned back when they got to the dentist's door. The degree of arousal required for adequate performance in the situation was so great that instead of being keyed up to do well they did not succeed at all in doing what they set out to do.

The development of pressure into stress is not just in relation to one particular event. It relates to the whole of our lives. If you work under pressure for long periods of time it can affect your performance in every area. You do not do your job as well as you might, and your relationships and your health suffer.

As you carry out your day-to-day activities, you need a degree of tension to help you perform adequately. If you are not concerned to get to work on time, for example, you would lie in bed, dawdle over breakfast, and arrive late for work. This would not do much for your chances of promotion or the boss's opinion of you. Nor would you get much work done. We put pressure on ourselves to pay bills, to drive in traffic, to voice our opinions when necessary, to express our displeasure, to complete work to deadlines, to rearrange our schedules when needed. We do many of these things every day and mostly without undue pressure. It is only when the degree of pressure which we experience is out of proportion, or our perceptions of it are out of proportion to the degree of action required, that it becomes unhealthy stress. It is at this point that a small problem such as a computer crash, or a jammed photocopier, can be the "straw that breaks the camel's back" and you plunge down the scale.

Over a period of time you may find that the degree of pressure seems to be out of proportion much of the time and your whole life begins to feel pressured and stressed. Work stress may spill over into home life and you feel generally tired and exhausted. You know you are not doing well and this increases the pressure. This is stress.

If you look again at the Human Function Curve with more detail added you will be able to distinguish where you are in relation to the way in which you are performing in your life relative to your degree of pressure or perceived pressure. Are you a good decision maker? Are you frustrated?

Diagram 2

Performance - Pressure

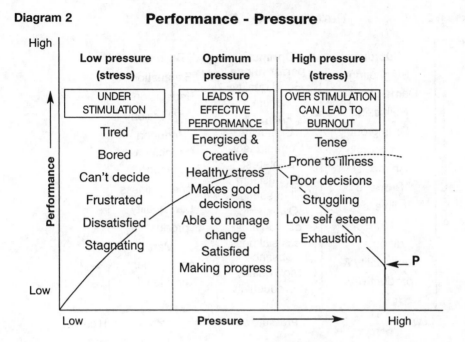

The term burnout is the phrase often used these days when we talk about job stress and it has become a major problem in many professional and non-professional occupations. Burnout is a gradual process in which once productive and committed workers lose all interest in their job or profession and this affects their creativity and motivation. Victims of burnout often experience physical and emotional exhaustion, total lack of interest in work, and detachment from fellow workers. Burnout can result from stress. Although burnout can strike anyone, the individuals most vulnerable are the ones who deal with people on a daily basis.

Certain professions are particularly vulnerable. These are health, care, law enforcement and teaching. Individuals in these groups should be particularly concerned about good stress management.

Diagram 3

Performance - Pressure

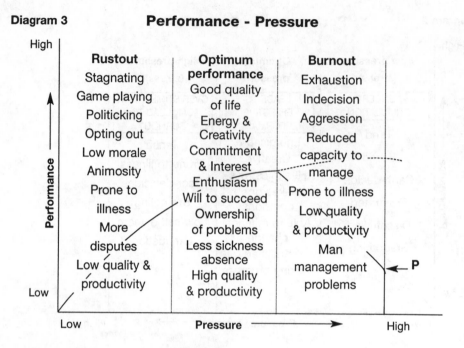

In which of these zones are you, most of the time?

Another important factor which influences where we are on the above curve is that the degree of stress which people prefer in their lives varies with each one of us. Most of us can cope with, and even enjoy, short-term high stress induced by competitive sports, a new relationship, birth of a baby, a new job, an exciting holiday. Situations such as these create stress of one kind or another and if we tried to avoid them our lives would be very boring.

Also our perceptions play an important part. Some of us perceive certain activities and events to be stressful, whilst other people enjoy the adrenaline buzz. For example, you may take giving presentations in your stride, or you may be like large numbers of people in the country who said they were more anxious about giving presentations than they were about death.

So why is it that some people get more stressed than others? Or that certain situations cause stress to one person but not to another? If I were able to take a poll of my readers at this point I am sure I would find an interesting list of things that people find stressful, and those they do not. But the most interesting thing would be that some of the same things would appear on both lists. You may work in a highly stressed environment and as you look at your colleagues you will notice that some of them appear to take it all in their stride, whilst others do not cope very well at all and have lots of sick leave, or suffer from psychological ill-health.

Diagram 4

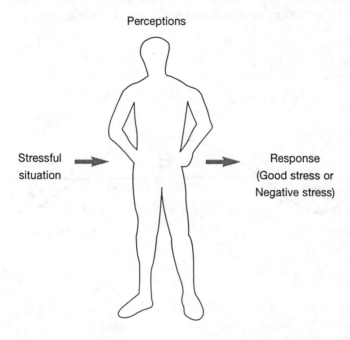

Perceptions

Stressful situation ➡️ ➡️ Response (Good stress or Negative stress)

The answer is to do with us. Our perceptions of a situation (what we say to ourselves about it) and the amount of adaptation energy we have as an individual, all affect whether or not a situation is likely to be stressful for us. I will talk about perceptions in a later chapter. For the moment let us look at adaptation energy.

Hans Selye[2] said that all of us only have so much "adaptation energy" and that each of us has a different amount. He talked about the three stages of stress, with the middle stage being the variable one according to the amount of this energy which each of us has.

A friend of mine, Mario Loulie[3], was brought up in South Africa. He has described to me beaches there where people go to have fun with the waves. There are no coral reefs or sandbars in South Africa, so huge rolling breakers, six feet or more in height,come rolling in to the beaches and the young people particularly like to go down to the beach and have fun with the waves. They stand at the edge of the sea and wait for a wave to come crashing over them.

When the first wave comes they have to be standing very firmly, or the force of the wave is likely to knock them off their feet. If that happens they have got to get back on their feet pretty quickly and re-stabilise themselves before the next wave comes. If they do not then a third wave may be upon them and they are going to need some help or they are likely to be swamped and pulled into the sea.

Stress is very like this, with three defined stages, each stronger than the previous one. They are the Alarm Stage, the Resistance Stage and the Exhaustion Stage.

Diagram 5

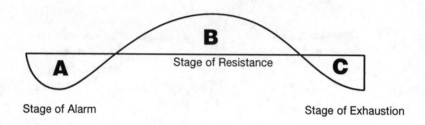

Stage of Alarm

Stage of Exhaustion

Alarm stage

This is the stage when we are at our best under stress. In response to difficult, dangerous or worrying situations the body acts in a typical way, keying us up to face the challenge. The nervous system generates a complex chain of chemical and biochemical responses which mobilise energy in a way which is described fully in Chapter 4. People have been known to perform tremendous feats of strength under stress, which would be unknown under normal circumstances, such as lifting a car to free someone trapped underneath.

This stage is perfectly healthy and the body is responding just as it is designed to do. After the appropriate response (flight or fight), the body activates another response to relax the body and it returns to normal. The alarm stage is usually short-lived.

This is the stage of challenge when we are in the "healthy tension" section of the Human Performance Curve. Added pressure at this stage triggers increased performance which is viewed as a challenge. You "pull out all the stops" to do well and when the pressure is over you return to the previous state. In this stage you do not take work problems home with you, you sleep well, and your health is good. When things go wrong you rise to the occasion, keep things in perspective and laugh off your problems. You often feel creative and dynamic, being able to think quickly, clearly and positively. Do you remember those days?

At this stage good stress management will keep you in balance and unless there are added problems or severe pressure over a long time you will remain healthy and be free of stress-related symptoms. The motto is at this stage is "Work hard and play hard".

It may be that it is a new job, or a young family, which are stretching and challenging you, and you get a buzz out of overcoming difficulties that arise. Your work is up to date, you have time for leisure activities and have no difficulties sleeping at nights[4]. In other words you are standing firm as the first wave of stress washes over you. If the stress goes on for a long period of time, however, or is very severe, you move into the second stage.

The adaptation stage

The second wave of stress needs you to have the ability to recover quickly because of the added pressures. It uses up a lot of physical and nervous energy as you try to keep in balance and perform well in spite of these, or because of the on-going nature of the stress. The responses which return the body to a normal state are not triggered automatically at this stage and long-term stress may set in. The length of time for which you can continue to perform well in your job, or balance life's many pressures, will vary for each person and has more to do with the person themselves than with the nature of the stress.

At this stage the body and mind can adapt to cope with the stressors and our symptoms may disappear, thus we may lose an important warning mechanism. There is a real danger that you may not yourself be aware of how stressed you are becoming.

You may notice yourself visiting the doctor more often as you draw on the body's stores of energy and they are not replaced quickly enough. The ailments themselves are usually minor and niggling rather than serious, but you find yourself taking pills and medication more often, relying on them to keep you going. You may also resort to "comfort tricks" to make life more pleasant, such as eating more, drinking (alcohol) more, and smoking more. You find yourself running out of patience at work and at home, becoming more touchy than normal. This is made worse because you do not have the energy you would like to get on top of everything. You feel helpless and hopeless and sometimes feel like you need a good cry, or want to hit out. It is in this stage that you begin to feel "pressured" and see no way out. You may know your behaviour is beginning to change and that other people are noticing. At this point good stress management techniques are very important to restore balance and help you return to Stage One.

If the stress continues, it begins to drain your physical and emotional energy. It gets harder to bounce back after a challenging event, working late to meet deadlines, or putting in extra effort to cope with something unexpected.

Lord Moran, personal physician to Winston Churchill, in his studies of shell-shocked soldiers, referred to adaptation energy as "courage". Every individual may inherit a different amount. Once it is gone the individual suffers from burnout. Senility in the elderly and shell-shock in young soldiers are alike in a sense. Both seem to result from having spent all one's adaptation energy.

Good stress management techniques are vital at this stage in order to help you return to the first stage, otherwise you will move into the exhaustion stage, because each of us only has so much "adaptation energy" to help us cope. The amount varies from individual to individual and is based on a lot of different factors, but one thing is sure and that is that if the stress continues over a long period of time then there will come a point when a small added pressure can be the "final straw" – you have run out of energy.

The exhaustion stage

This is the stage when the third wave is about to hit you and could pull you under. All the body's resources have been used up, mentally and physically. If you do not do something about the degree of stress you are under now you are going to be very ill indeed. This, of course, is the burnout phase which is the result of prolonged exposure to factors which cause stress.

It is the danger zone. In this stage you feel very ill, physically and mentally. Your relationships suffer and you are likely to find yourself getting out of touch with what is going on. The changes in behaviour which were evident in the adaptation stage are now obvious to everyone, often more so than yourself. You become frightened that life will always be like this. Illness and changes in behaviour are chronic and can no longer be disguised. At this stage long-term absence from work and even bed-rest are necessary to allow the body to regain its equilibrium. Good stress management at this stage is vital before severe illness develops which may be life-threatening. You are likely to depend on comfort tricks such as alcohol, pills and cigarettes to try to help you cope.

This third stage is the one to be avoided at all costs.

Summary

In the alarm stage you can use the stress management techniques which you will find in this book to help you keep alert and aware, ready to handle further stress, and you will remain healthy in body and mind. You still have lots of adaptation energy at this stage and may not see the need for stress management unless you become aware of reaching the second stage.

In the adaptation stage you need to think much more carefully about your stress, and make stress-management techniques a priority in your life to avoid passing into the exhaustion stage. You also need to be aware of the fact that you seem to be coping well and may have lost touch with your alarm bell.

At the exhaustion stage you will need drastic stress management techniques to help you get back to normal. You may even need some outside help. If you recognise yourself as having reached this stage then it is important that you take and use stress-management advice so that serious stress-related illness can be prevented.

No one is immune, because this is the result of the body's natural reaction to a perceived threat. It happens at a level which is not in conscious awareness. This knowledge will help your understanding of stress. But knowing about stress is not enough. You have to do something about it to prevent stress-related illness.

For many years I worked in the Health Service and talked to many nurses, doctors, and people in other professions concerned with patient care. Many of them were in positions where they needed to give advice to others concerning health matters, often stress-related. A pattern that I noticed in some staff was that they did not follow the advice themselves. Whilst they said the right things, they themselves worked long, tiring hours without a break, ate unhealthy diets, smoked excessively, and generally acted as though they were immune to stress. It seemed as though they believed that as they knew about stress it would not affect them; as if having a bottle of antibiotic pills in the cupboard would be sufficient to ward off an infection. But no matter what your work is, you are as vulnerable as anyone else to the stresses and strains of modern living. It is not knowing about, but doing something about, stress which is important and in the next chapter you will begin to discover what it is you need to do and why it works.

References

1. Nixon, Dr. Peter (1987) Senior Consultant Cardiologist, Charing Cross Hospital, London. Quoted in Webster, P (1990)"Your Stress Management In Teaching", New Education Press, London.

2. Selye H (1950) *Stress*, Montreal, Octa

3. Loulie, Mario, Manchester Leadership Alliance, Northwich, Cheshire.

4. Mills, Sandra H (1990) *Stress Management for Teachers*, Framework Press, Lancaster.

chapter three

Working to live, or living to work?

Some of the people that I teach about stress are university students. Many of them have come straight from school. When we come to talk about stress they are often quite cynical until I give them a stress questionnaire to fill in. Some of them find that they already have quite serious stress-related problems linked to exam pressure, and poor lifestyle. Their comments to me are usually along the lines of, "I thought stress was something that only executives suffered from. I did not realise that it could affect young people too." Their interest in stress had been purely academic until then.

What about you? Do you think you might be under stress, or are you reading this book in order to be able to help someone else? Is stress something that you should be concerned about?

Joe

With the ease borne of long practice Joe activated his printer, leaned back and closed his eyes, letting the document he had just completed spill onto the out tray. One more assignment completed, two more to go. It is true there were only two weeks to go to the deadline but he reckoned if he burned the midnight oil most nights he'd get them completed. He was young and fit and could usually rise to the challenge of a night or two without sleep. The exams were something else and he wouldn't think about that just now!

Being at university was great, he really enjoyed the clubs and social activities which were available, and he'd met loads of girls. At this point he stopped and enjoyed the tingling feeling which resulted when he thought of Louise whom he was now seeing regularly. He'd never met anyone quite like her before and was desperate to spend as much time with her as possible and see where their relationship might go. He was determined to see off the competition although this brought added pressure to his life at the moment which he would prefer to avoid.

So he was seeing Louise most evenings, then trying to study late into the night at least once during the week, plus the time he was able to spend in the library between lectures on some days. Mealtimes were practically non-existent – usually a hasty burger from the student canteen at lunch time, sometimes only crisps and an apple on days when lectures spanned the lunch break.

Evening meals were something else again. When he and two others had moved into this flat they had drawn up a rota for cooking, cleaning, shopping, etc. It sounded great. This had lasted exactly four weeks – once fully into the semester it had been every man for himself and their tiny kitchen was littered with half-consumed cans of beans, empty take-away cartons, ageing packets of sliced bread and opened packets of breakfast cereals. Their evening meal was usually taken on the hoof and was always the easiest option. Usually he managed to grab something on his way through the flat before meeting Louise, or he would bring in a take-away on his way back from lectures.

He occasionally worried about his lifestyle, particularly since that lecture they'd had on stress in the second year. But he was young and healthy he did not reckon that stress would get to him until he was an executive. They were the people that developed ulcers from stress, weren't they?

Oh well, back to the computer and this assignment. At least there was light at the end of the tunnel. Graduation was only six months away and he'd be able to have a nice long holiday before getting down to job hunting. He would miss University but it would be great to have some money in his pocket, and with a steady job he could afford somewhere better to live. He'd already begun to hint to Louise that they might move in together.

Joe thought back to the work placement he had done during the second year of this sandwich degree course. He had obtained a position with a large manufacturing company as personal assistant to their Head of Marketing. His role had been to mastermind several small projects, closely supervised by his boss. He had written some marketing literature and designed some leaflets, as well as collating company information and statistics. He wouldn't mind trying to get something similar later this year.

He was quite looking forward to the chances of getting a job, his business degree should stand him in good stead there, and then working life would be a doddle after University, wouldn't it?

Joe is putting off and refusing to think about the effects of his late nights, tight deadlines and erratic lifestyle on his stress levels, believing that because he is young stress is not a problem. If you are reading this book then perhaps your interest in stress is more immediate. If it is personal do you seriously want to do anything about it? Before you read on I'd like to ask you to answer a couple of questions.

"What, for you, is the most important thing in your life?"

"What matters most to you in all the world?"

In other words, what are your priorities? People's priorities generally fall into three categories: family, work and personal. If you have never seriously thought about your priorities before, take a moment now and write down in the space overleaf what are your most important goals in these areas.

Family/relationships ....

Work/career ....

Personal development/health ....

Knowing what is most important to you will help you recognise whether your life is in balance. When the chips are down, what counts most in your life? What do you want to achieve in each of these areas, and is any one of them more important than another? Is it your family, your partner, your children, or is your career and personal advancement your highest priority? What about yourself and your personal desires to be healthy, to travel, to study for a qualification: where do any of these kind of wishes figure in your list of priorities?

Jean-Dominique Bauby, former editor of *Elle* magazine in Paris, suffered a massive stroke in 1995. After several weeks in a coma he regained consciousness but was unable to move any muscle, except those controlling the left eyelid. Yet his mind was as alert and active as ever. This condition is known as locked-in syndrome. Where a lesser mortal might have given up and waited for death, he decided to write a book, dictating it by blinking to indicate each individual character, from an alphabet read out to him by a devoted assistant. The book is called *The Diving Bell and the Butterfly*[1] and in it Jean-Do, as he was known to his friends, reflected on his life, his exciting job, the advertising agency he had started, the many famous people he had met, the great meals he had eaten, and realised that it was all as dust. His love for his children, and their love for him was what mattered most, together with the enduring support of his true friends. He had 15 months to savour and appreciate them all, and to realise the depth of their fondness for him, an appreciation which made the fact of his existence feel worthwhile. Many of us think that we have no time for such niceties and miss never having these insights until it is all too late. The important things in our lives are often taken for granted and too often neglected. Yet it is an appreciation of these factors that help us to realise just what it is all for, why we are working in the first place, and where we need to put our major effort.

Michelle was the head teacher of a small country school. She had a full teaching responsibility as well as her management role, and was teetering on the edge of a breakdown when I met her. She had been enjoying the challenge of managing the school, but was finding that it was absorbing all her time and her energy, particularly keeping up with all the statutory requirements and mountains of paperwork. There always seemed to be something new to deal with.

Michelle's family included her husband, who himself had a lot of job pressure, a young daughter, and an elderly parent at the other end of the country. She told me that after attending a stress management course she realised for the first time that her family, particularly her daughter were getting a very raw deal. "I'm there to feed her and attend to her physical needs", she told me, " ferry her to Brownies and dancing class, but we do not have time to spend together as mother and daughter should. I spend more time and energy on my job, than I do on my family," she said. She also was realising that her own health was beginning to suffer. She was suffering from hurry sickness and she found herself running everywhere.

From that moment she began to set dedicated time aside for both her husband and her daughter. She started to accept that she was only a human being, and that human beings are not all-powerful; they have limitations. She focused on making the best possible use of the time she had available because she did not have much of it: she concentrated on quality time rather than quantity time. This helped her own stress too as she turned her attention to matters outside work. She then had more energy for her work and could think more clearly when she went back to it on a Monday morning. She also had less indigestion, and fewer colds, and as an added bonus had found that giving up drinking coffee helped her relax more and stop running everywhere.

Michelle pulled herself back from the brink just in time. But many are like Frank, a colleague, who changed careers in his forties and became a further education teacher after a life in the army. He so enjoyed his new field of work that he threw himself into it heart and soul. He turned his spare room into a study and when he was not at work he was in the study, marking work, planning lessons, devising work schemes. He put a lot of hours into extra-curricular activities, such as the college drama group, and was also active in his professional association, being elected chairman of the local branch. He became very well known, everyone liked him, and frequently rang him up with problems and queries. You might wonder where, in all this, he found time for his wife. He did not. Fortunately they had no children, because one day he came home from work and found his wife had packed her bags. She had had enough, and left him to make a new life and look for a partner who would have time for her as well as work, leaving Frank devastated. He became aware, all too late, what his dedication to his job had cost him.

Not only is there a danger that we might lose things that are precious to us, but we live our lives out of balance with our priorities and unless we are aware of this we do not realise where our stress is coming from. The body can cope with mismatches of this kind for short periods of time, but in the long term severe stress can result. This happened quite a lot in the National Health Service in the early 90s, the years of the NHS reforms, when many staff were being promoted into management posts and given complete responsibility for their own personnel and budgets. These jobs were very tempting, with their increased responsibility and higher salaries. As a training officer in those days, I worked closely with many of the staff who had taken these posts. Some of them thrived, but there were others who showed signs of quite severe stress. When I analysed this with them, what we discovered was that not only was the job stressful in itself, but they had lost sight of their priorities. Many found the transition uncomfortable because they had chosen their work in order to be a part of a caring profession (nurses for example). They began their careers with unusual enthusiasm and idealism, believing that theirs is a very special profession. Their new management roles meant that they lost the opportunity to have direct contact with patients and had to spend much of their time balancing budgets, managing staff, and making often unpopular management decisions, which were contrary to the decisions they might have made in their caring role. Their new role had to be very much focused on the bottom line. I remember the anguish of one such manager, Marian, who had been one of our finest and most respected ward sisters. Her dilemma was about the use of very expensive and scarce nursing equipment for her ward. In the old days she would have requested what she wanted on the grounds of patient need and it would have been provided. Now she had to manage her own budget which was already overspent. She had a tremendous battle with the management whose bottom line was money not patient care. The outcome was that she took early retirement and the Health Service lost one of its best nurses. Her commitment to patient welfare could not be reconciled with the need to balance the books. She has this in common with Elizabeth Perle McKenna, a publishing executive for 20 years who gave it all up when she found her private life was becoming submerged by her professional life. She found herself checking a list of achievements: "But as I proceeded down the list, I felt less and less good about my accomplishments because they involved more and more trade-offs in some inner valuing system."[2]

Are you living your life in such a way that you are in harmony with your priorities? Are you living to work, or working to live? So many of us do not stop to think what our priorities are, and what we're doing it all for. We have to rediscover our priorities and achieve a balance, or our reason for working so hard will not make any sense. So my second question to you is: "Are you living your life in such a way that it is obvious where your priorities lie, and are you are happy that you've got your priorities right?".

Just picture this. When your life has come to an end, as all our lives must, and you are lying on your death bed, with all your family gathered round to say goodbye, as you raise your head from the pillow to say a final word to them all, what will your final words be? Will they be, "Oh, I do wish I'd had more time to spend in the office/factory/school/hospital/shop etc.?" I think not. But do not let your final words be those of regret that you have not spent time with the most important people in your life, or found the time to achieve your life's ambition.

"But", you might say, "if I'm to get anywhere in my job I have to put in long hours and take work home. If I do not then my income will be affected and the family will suffer." This may be true and you may see yourself with no choice at the moment as you build up a business or a career. If this is so, then discuss it with your family and set limits on your time. You may even need to timetable some of your family life to make sure that you give it some of your time. Also make sure that when you are with them it is quality time. An hour spent actively doing something with a family member, and really communicating with them, as opposed to just talking, is worth four hours slumped in front of the TV, or hunched over a computer in the corner. You may be physically with your family whilst you write that report, or mark those books, but you are not available to them, and that does not count as time with them.

It is important too to be aware of whether you really need to put in those extra hours. Some of us put this pressure on ourselves, we do not see ourselves as workaholics and would refute any such suggestion, saying, "I need to put in these hours if I'm to do my job properly!" The trouble is, for some people, the more we do, the more there is to do. It is a form of Parkinson's Law. Running my own business helped me to recognise this tendency in myself. I would work most evenings and weekends. In the beginning I had to work hard to launch the business and get a level of income that would support me. But it became a way of life and as the work came in I found that by continuing to work hard I could get even more work. What I then found was that it was hard to stop, to recognise the point at which enough was enough and I could allow myself to work hard during the day and find time for myself in the evenings. I found it hard to remember what it was I used to do when I was not working!

You may need to enlist family and friends to help you do this. Get them to be tough with you and drag you away from your computer or your books. It can be hard to do this if you are a Type A person. Type As are the ones that are more prone to stress than Type Bs. Type A and Type B personalities have been described by Professors Friedman and Rosenman[3] who discovered that, particularly among white collar, professional and managerial groups, this personality type was more likely to suffer from stress related illness, particularly heart disease. They are the people who are very hard-driving, over-assertive, ambitious, time-conscious, and fast-moving. They are most likely to take work home, and work long hours, actively trying to get ahead in the shortest possible time. Unfortunately, although most organisations like to have some Type A people amongst their executives, research has shown that they are the ones most likely to suffer from high levels of sickness. Friedman and Rosenman called this coronary prone behaviour.

Type A people are intensely competitive and constantly try to score points. They are impatient, and pushed by an excessive sense of time urgency. They frequently do more than one thing at a time, move rapidly and often, and can not bear to wait in queues. For them a computer breakdown is a serious disaster to be compared only with the sinking of the *Titanic*.

They can be hard taskmasters on themselves, setting themselves targets and goals in all areas of their lives as well as in their work. This can make them aggressive and driven. I met one Type A person who, when recovering from a physical condition, was told by his doctor to get out and walk every day. He then set himself a target as to how far he should walk, and tried to beat it on a daily basis, competing with himself and losing the whole point of the activity. Not only that but when the pain was too much and he did not beat his target he was depressed and angry with himself.

Type A people rarely pause long enough to think about the effect stress is having on them. They thrive on it, probably because their bodies manufacture greater quantities than normal of noradrenalin, the stress hormone associated with feelings of confidence and elation. Noradrenalin is found more often in men than in women. The mental and physical highs produced by this hormone lead to what doctors term stress addiction and the addict purposely seeks out high-stress situations and indulges in stress-inducing behaviour, becoming hooked on stress and victimised by his or her own responses.

Overachievers are particularly at risk. They generally will not give in to illness or fatigue and find it hard to refuse the excessive demands made on them They are perfectionists by nature, often driven by fear of falling short of their own expectations of themselves. One significant characteristic is that they place the needs of others before their own, yet find it hard to express their deepest feelings. It may be that they find it easier to do this through working hard, using the excuse "I'm doing it for them". Sadly they are usually unable accurately to assess their personal limitations and admit that they are vulnerable.

Type B people on the other hand are more cooperative and look for opportunities to work together with people rather than score points over them, or win. They tend to be more laid back in their attitude to life generally. They can accept delays and be more forgiving of mistakes.

The rushing and competing of Type A people is likely to lead to frequent frustration which demands so much of their bodies that they put their heart and circulatory system at risk. They are also likely to be the type of people who do not suffer fools gladly and their relationships may become strained. This kind of behaviour is more serious if it is done unconsciously.   With the realisation of what you are doing comes the opportunity to change. However, hurrying and competition are not an issue when they are appropriate to the activity in hand, because they do not constantly drain your energy and there is opportunity to recover.

When you recognise yourself as a Type A you can do something about it   You can deliberately copy the Type B personality, adopting some of the characteristics of a more relaxed lifestyle. You may not be able to change your underlying personality, but you can change the way you express it. This may mean deliberately curtailing long working hours, taking frequent short breaks and longer holidays, and generally managing the way you live, looking for opportunities to switch off .

You will find a questionnaire to help you recognise Type A behaviour at the back of this book and the questions that are asked will give you clues to what you need to do to change. There are people who combine some of qualities of both these personality types. Your individual score will give you an indication of whether you incline more towards being Type A or Type B.

Whatever your personality type it is possible that you are in danger of accepting stress-related symptoms as a norm and an inevitable part of life - that is until your health is affected. The principal way you can guard against becoming ill through too much stress is to recognise early signals and to know how far you can push yourself without incurring more serious symptoms. This means being more sensitive to your bodily functions and emotions at a level which is often beyond awareness, until you stop rushing and take notice. You need to learn to identify your own personal stress profile so that you can act before major illnesses take a hold.

We need to do this to safeguard others too, because stress can be like a virus. When one person becomes stressed others around them start acting stressed too. You need to be able to recognise this stress in others. It can sometimes be difficult to discover the source of this stress. It might be a manager, or other key figure in the workplace, or it might be someone with a lesser role in the organisation, an office junior, a caretaker, someone whose behaviour is affecting those around them. They pass their stresses on to their colleagues, in the same way that they might pass on a virus. Look around your place of work. If you detect signs of stress there, is it possible to work out where the stress is coming from?

It could be that the problem is at home. Is one of the family members so stressed that they are affecting the rest of the family? Stress-related illness is often seen in children as a result of parents' stress - disharmony between parents, redundancy, bereavement, etc. which they have not the emotional maturity to cope with. Children's stress often takes the form of illnesses which may not be recognised as warning signs of stress, eczema and asthma for example as well as the more common emotional and behavioural problems such as bed-wetting or tantrums.

Check your own stress levels and discover whether you might be the person who is the originator of stress in your home or work environment. Take measures to handle it well so that you do not pass it on. Make sure that you are living according to your values and priorities. Check also your reactions to other peoples' stress. Employ good stress management techniques and make sure that the stress stops with you. Halt it before the stress virus passes through the entire work environment or family network.

In the following chapters you will discover how stress can trigger physical and mental illnesses, and learn some practical ways in which you can intervene to prevent stress.

References

1. Bauby, Jean-Do (1997) *The Diving Bell and the Butterfly*, (Fourth Estate) quoted by Charles Handy in *Management Today*, September 1997.

2. McKenna, Elizabeth Perle (1997) *When Work Does not Work Anymore*, Simon and Schuster.

3. Friedman, MT and Rosenman, R H (1974) *Type A Behaviour and Your Heart*, Knopf, New York, NY.

4. Kirsta, Alix (1986) *The Handbook of Stress Survival*, Unwin Paperbacks, London.

chapter four

There's a cave man in all of us!

Man, homo sapiens, has been around a long time, evolving over many thousands of years and, in order to survive, has needed to respond quickly and physically to many dangers, such as wild animals and warring tribes. Generally the response was a desire to stand and fight, to run away, or to freeze on the spot until the danger had passed. This has come to be known as the flight/fight or the flight/fight/freeze reaction. We all still have this hormonal and chemical defence mechanism, but for the most part it is not as much use in today's lifestyle as it was when our ancestors lived in caves.

My story

There were times when I wondered whether I was completely out of my mind. Here I was, a normal healthy adult, who could have been spending her holidays lazing on a Mediterranean beach, worrying about nothing more than what time to go and eat. Instead of that I was sweating aboard the deck of a 27 foot yacht in filthy jeans and sweater, straining to raise the mast so that we could check the electrical fittings, rigging, etc. ready for the new season. John and I had been married for less than a year and it was a second marriage for both of us. I knew John lived and breathed boats and so far I'd found sailing a new and challenging hobby. I was reserving judgement about anything more than that especially at the moment.

The boat was standing on our drive. It had a deep keel and was on a road trailer, which meant that the level of the deck was about the height of our first floor bedroom windows. We climbed aboard using ladders, and now here we were using a home-made pulley to get the mast up. I was standing in the stern with my back to John taking some of the weight of the mast as he heaved on the pulley. I hadn't been too keen on that pulley. It was made from a pair of step-ladders roped together and looked decidedly unsafe to me. But it wasn't until there was a deathly silence, followed by a weird, grunting noise that I realised my fears had been well-grounded. At first John was nowhere to be seen, but when I looked over the side of the boat, I saw him lying on the concrete driveway, curled into a little ball, making a very strange noise which I learned later was his attempt to re-inflate his lungs. He had been catapulted off the deck of the boat when his pulley slipped, and on landing on the driveway had had all the breath knocked out of his body.

I can not describe the next few moments except to say that my brain froze. The sight of him in this position completely panicked me . I was up on the boat and couldn't immediately see how I could get down to help him as he had knocked his access ladder away in his fall. In my fright I'd completely forgotten that I'd climbed up at the other side of the boat on another ladder! The only thing that came to mind immediately was that he mustn't be moved in case he had broken his neck, or back, and so I stood on the deck of the boat and shouted to him, 'Do not move! Do not move.' The poor man couldn't have moved at that moment to save his life! This was me, normally cool-headed and first-aid trained, and I couldn't put two thoughts together! I could only shout for help.

Eventually a neighbour heard my cries for help and took control of the situation, ringing for an ambulance. I gathered my wits together and provided blankets to make him comfortable until the ambulance arrived (there was no external bleeding). Fortunately the only damage done was internal bruising. (He didn't walk properly for several weeks but it didn't put him off sailing!) For my own part I re-took some First Aid training and have carried on sailing. Ten years on I am still finding it exciting and challenging.

For a few minutes, the stress response rooted me to the spot and, instead of responding resourcefully and planning a course of action, I was frozen into the inactivity of which I was very ashamed later. What I was demonstrating was the ultimate in stress response.

The stressors which modern man and woman face can not always be dealt with by a physical reaction. Our defence mechanisms find little outlet in our more civilised lifestyle. Our bodies want to run away or to stand and fight the danger. But it is not socially acceptable to punch someone on the nose, nor can we usually run away and hide whenever things are not going our way.

Fighting or running away was useful for our ancestors, as was freezing on the spot. You can stay quiet, yet vigilant, for a long time, until the danger has passed. The stresses and strains that modern man faces are no longer wild animals, or warring tribes, but your body acts as though they are. You produce exactly the same reaction. The body wants to fight or run away, or can sometimes freeze and do nothing useful. Today's stressors are more complicated than wild animals. You cannot hide or run away from a pile of bills, unemployment, or redundancy, although you usually wish you could. These stressors need you to think clearly and make sensible decisions in order to resolve them, which is often the last thing you feel able to do. Your body and mind are urging you to run away and hide in a nice dark cave, or producing feelings of anger making you want to storm and shout and hit something, or somebody! We react in the same way to every situation that our brain interprets as stress, when what we really need is rational action. You can only take rational action when you have taken control of your mind and its response to the stress. You can then begin to think clearly.

Today, when we have to get ourselves out of physical danger in a hurry, this same response is still useful, and is generally quite efficient. For example if you are crossing the road and you notice a fast car bearing down on you, you get yourself out of the way and generally find yourself on the pavement, breathing fast, heart pumping, and legs feeling very wobbly. In an extreme situation you may even feel quite faint.

One thing you do not do is to stand in the middle of the road and say, "Oh, dear, there is a car coming. I need to get out of the way. I'd better tell my legs to move fast, and I'll give them some more haemoglobin to carry some extra oxygen to my muscles. I'll tell my heart to beat faster too, to pump the blood to the muscles. Whilst I'm about it I'll get the liver to produce some more glucose for extra energy, I'll sweat a bit more to cool myself down. I'll also switch off my digestive processes, and any other system I'm not using at the moment, including my higher brain, so as to channel my energies and bodily resources to my immediate need. It would be pretty useful if I could also empty my bowel and bladder so as to lighten the load too."

You do not consciously do this, but that is what happens in the split second before you find yourself once again on the pavement. This, and much more, takes place outside of your conscious awareness because of the action of the nervous system. During this time your brain (cortical activity) is suspended and you function on your pea brain which acts instinctively. This is why we do stupid things, or have irrational, even crazy thoughts at these times, like my response to John's accident.

Alternatively, you may find yourself able to cope surprisingly well with a one-off disaster, but the daily grind of a dissatisfying job, working in unpleasant surroundings, money worries, family worries, threat of redundancy, inability to find employment, to name but a few of today's stressors, are the things that get you down. You may have risen to the challenge when you discovered an outbreak of fire. You did all the right things including operating the fire alarm, finding a fire extinguisher and clearing the building. Afterwards you congratulated yourself on your swift action and clear thinking. But what do you do about that unpleasant colleague who refuses to take full share of the work and causes enormous problems for everyone else, including you? You can not run away or physically fight in that situation. Wouldn't it be great if a quick squirt with a fire extinguisher would sort them out? What if you are not getting on with your mother-in-law and she insists on giving interfering advice in your family affairs? Punching her on the nose is not going to solve anything, quite the reverse.

This bodily reaction is the same for all of us. It is a normal human reaction and is not an indication that we are weak, or going mad.

Diagram 6

Changes occurring when brain becomes aware of danger

"Panic button" is pushed

Warning messages sent along nerves

Stress response switched on

Mind alert or confused (higher brain switched off, you act instinctively, often irrationally

Adrenaline pumped through system to alert major organs and switch them into over-drive

Less saliva, dry mouth

Breathing rate faster and shallower as oxygen taken in more quickly

Nostrils and air passages widen

Muscles tense as they prepare for action

Heart beats faster and irregularly.

Blood pressure rises

Blood diverted to muscles

Blood clotting ability increased to prepare for possible injury

Liver releases glucose for energy

Sweating increases to cool body

Sphincter muscles of bowel and bladder contract and natural rhythm switched off

White blood cell count depressed and ability to fight infection and disease inhibited (to conserve resources)

Natural appetites, e.g. hunger and sexual desire, diminished

Digestive juices switched off

The stresses and strains of modern life are ongoing too. It seems like there is always something to worry about, or it takes time for difficulties to go away. The stress response is switched on all the time, as if you have been put in a cage with one of the wild animals and cannot find a way out. Or it may be low-level stress, vague worries and anxieties that are always in the back of your mind, as if you sense that there is a wild animal somewhere out there and it is going to come for you sooner or later.

Factfile No. 1.

Some physical signs and symptoms of stress:

Mild or severe headaches

Itching or skin rash

Constant tiredness

Dizzy spells, faintness

Twitching or trembling

Upset stomach, indigestion, feelings of nausea, stomach ache

Constipation or diarrhoea

Aches, pains or cramps

Heart beating faster, or harder

Palpitations or panic attacks

Lack of appetite

Frequent indigestion or heartburn

Tendency to sweat for no good reason

Nausea

Breathlessness without exertion

Hair loss

Of course it is not only the body that is affected by stress. There are three typical mental reactions. You either become very focused and go all out for what you want, even at the expense of other people, or you become confused and forgetful and find it hard to think straight. The third reaction is to freeze and do nothing and become mentally rooted to the spot. At times of major disasters such as an aeroplane fire these three behaviours are clearly demonstrated. Some people fight their way out of the plane, unaware that they are treading on other people. Others do stupid things like trying to get at their duty frees before leaving the blazing plane, obstructing exits as they do so. Still others do nothing at all and sit frozen in their seats whilst pandemonium breaks out around them. Which of these reactions might be typical of you, do you think? Are you aware of how your mind behaves when it is under stress? Which psychological reactions have you noticed? These reactions may not be just temporary either. Some recent research has indicated that long-term stress may shrink part of the brain that keeps people intelligent. One of the chemicals, hydrocortisone, released when under stress has a special affinity for a part of the brain called the hippocampus, which helps us learn and remember. Sapolsky[1] found that in rats months of stress shrink the hippocampus permanently. Now he thinks the same thing may happen in humans. Brain shrinkage was found in a high proportion of human subjects studied who had high levels of hydrocortisone.

Factfile No. 2

Psychological signs and symptoms of stress:

Feel as though you can not cope

Can not concentrate

Can not unwind

You are more snappy and irritable than usual

Tearful

Worrying unnecessarily

Have no interest and are easily discouraged

Can not get to sleep, or wake up in the night

Lost interest in sex

Energy levels are low/feeling tired

Feel as though you are a failure

Difficulty in making decisions

Loss of interest in other people

A feeling that other people are "getting at you"

Loss of sense of humour

Dread of the future

A feeling of having no one to confide in

Difficulty in concentrating

Want to be on your own more

Feeling angry and want to hit something

On a very "short fuse" and impatient

Inability to communicate well

Loss of ability to discriminate and judge even everyday situations accurately

Inability to feel or express any emotions, a sense of being on "automatic pilot"

Constantly changing your mind

Memory block/loss of short term memory

Lost for words

Inhibitions and anxiety when faced with every day challenges

Restlessness and frustration

Feelings of guilt

Feelings of shame

Factfile No. 3

Behavioural signs and symptoms of stress:

(It is useful to recognise that the physical and psychological manifestations of stress
  exhibit themselves in the behaviour too.)

Nodding off during meetings, or social gatherings

Moving in tense jerky way, and reacting nervously or irritably to everyday sounds

Using "props" more than usual -cigarettes, alcohol, pills, coffee, for example

Talking too fast, too loud or aggressively, swearing

Interrupting others or talking over them

Not listening, and arguing for the sake of it

Emotional outbursts and over-reactions

Craving for food when under pressure

Nail biting

Inability to sit still without fidgeting

Dietary problems

Clenching fists/jaw

Nervous habits - drumming fingers, grinding teeth, hunching shoulders, picking at
facial skin and fingernails, tapping feet, twisting and touching hair

Lack of exercise

Accidents and unsafe behaviour at work

Marital and family problems

Consistently feeling and acting out of character

Repeated outbursts

(These last two are significant warnings and if this behaviour is repeated over long
periods it may indicate serious problems.)

Think back to the last time you were aware of being stressed. Can you remember what it
felt like? How did your body feel? Did you get a headache for example? Were the palms
of your hands sweaty? I hope you are beginning to get a picture of why your body and
mind behave so strangely under stress and remembering how this feels for you.

In the short term this body and mind reaction is very useful it allows you to make a quick
response in a disaster situation. It is also a pretty good way to get you keyed up for
optimum performance. When you have to study for exams, for example, the fact that you
feel anxious is the thing that makes you cut out some of your socialising and study a bit
harder. Then the stress passes once you have sat your exams, and particularly when you
know you have passed. The stress response is switched off and your body returns to

normal.

Diagram 7

Bodily changes which occur when the stress response is switched off

Mind becomes more tranquil

Hormone production decreases

Breathing rate decreases as less oxygen is needed

Heart rate slows down

Muscles relax

Sweating decreases markedly

It is when the stresses are ongoing that the problems arise. The stress response is then switched on continuously, adrenaline is being produced all the time and your system is permanently in overdrive although you may not be aware of it. This is when stress becomes dangerous because it is producing wear and tear on your system which leads to physical, or even psychological, illness.

Shallow breathing might have become a habit and your brain may be being depleted of oxygen as a result. You may be aware of your heart beating faster and irregularly. You may recognise this as occasional palpitations, even when your body is at rest, and may have suffered the occasional panic attack, which is rapid shallow breathing accompanied by palpitations.

Are you sweating more? What are your bodily functions like? Are you constipated, or do you have the reverse problem, even an irritable bowel? Is your body giving you normal messages about hunger? Or are you missing meals and are you unaware of feeling hungry? On the other hand you may find yourself overeating, even bingeing at times. What is your physical resistance like? Can you throw off coughs and colds, or do you succumb to everything that is being passed round the office or the classroom, etc?

As you think about the way your body is designed to react in a stressful situation you will be able to see why you get the symptoms that you do, and why it is important to do something about the way your body is responding, even if you cannot do anything about the stress, to avert more serious problems.

Physical and mental illness of varying degrees are the result of uncontrolled stress. If the stress response is continually switched on, adrenaline is being produced more or less continuously. You might even get to like that feeling, particularly if you are one of the people whose mind becomes more alert under stress.

However, long-term damage is likely to result if the body and mind are in a continual state of readiness for danger. Think about it. If the digestive juices are switched off on a more or less permanent basis your food will not be digested properly. Indigestion is likely to be the first thing you notice, and this may lead on to peptic or duodenal ulcers. If your bowel is responding to danger signals you are likely to suffer from constipation, diarrhoea, irritable bowel syndrome or ulcerative colitis.

Often it is the heart and circulatory system which are most noticeably affected. Blood clotting ability is increased under stress, which is useful for coping with short-term danger, but when this is happening continually it could cause problems. This of course leads to the increased risk of stroke. If your heart is working overtime pumping blood to your organs you are likely to notice this as palpitations and if it is accompanied by rapid, shallow breathing you may interpret this as a panic attack, or even fear that you are having a heart attack. This would be particularly worrying if you were also suffering from pains in the chest or down the arms.

Factfile No. 4

List of ailments recognised to have a stress background:

Physical Illness

Heart attack (coronary thrombosis), strokes

High blood pressure

Headaches and migraine

Certain types of cancer

Gastrointestinal disorders (e.g. heartburn, ulcers, colitis)

Asthma

Diabetes mellitus

Multiple sclerosis

Hay fever and allergies

Pruritis (intense itching)

Skin disorders

Rheumatoid arthritis

Menstrual difficulties

Alopecia (hair loss, especially in women)

Back pain

Hyperthyroidism (overactive thyroid gland)

Tuberculosis

Impotence and sexual disorders

Constipation

Colitis

Digestive disorders

Muscular aches and pains

Factfile No. 5

List of mental problems likely to have a stress background:

Depression

Anxiety

Persecution complex (paranoia)

Sapolsky[2] says "your heart is just a dumb, simple, mechanical pump and your blood vessels are nothing more exciting than hoses". This means that those people who are constantly activating the stress response are going to wear out their hoses, their cardiovascular system. Recognising what stress is doing to you physically is the first step in taking action to do something about it. In subsequent chapters you will learn what it is you need to do and how to do it.

References

1. Sapolsky, Robert M of Stamford University, USA, quoted in "Second Opinion: stress for success", Forbes FYI March 13, 1995 v.155 n6 ps67(3).

2. Sapolsky, Robert M (1994) *Why Zebras Don't Get Ulcers*, Freeman, N.Y.

chapter five

The best way to eat an elephant is one bite at a time

The stress response is not just one event, but a process or a series of events, each one triggering the next. The earlier you take action to prevent or control the stress the easier it is to prevent a full-blown stress reaction.

Trisha

"Good-night, Trisha." It was her manager on his way home at the end of the day.

"Good-night, Ken."

Trisha listened to his footsteps dying away down the corridor and looked at her watch, it was five-thirty. She looked at the pile of papers on her desk. How she longed to just sweep them all into the bin and follow Ken out to the car park. Instead of that she knew she had at very least another hour's work before her.

She felt the familiar twinge of a headache starting at the base of her skull and rummaged in her desk drawer for her bottle of headache tablets.

Some of the other staff of the personnel department had already gone home and there were sounds of others packing up preparatory to doing the same. Filing cabinets were being opened and closed and doors being locked. "Why me? Why am I the only one who needs to work late? It is so unfair!" she wailed.

Trisha's job was to prepare contracts of employment for newly-appointed staff. This was a large organisation and new staff were being appointed almost on a daily basis. The quality standards which had been set meant that the organisation aimed to get contracts out to new staff within two weeks of their appointment. Trisha regularly worked overtime in order to achieve this standard. In theory she should be able to work flexibly and take time off when the work was easier, but somehow she never got round to this. She felt guilty if she was in the office later than anyone else, and even when she took a lunch break. She had a twisted idea that by doing this she might show everyone how hard she worked, but no one seemed to have noticed so far.

She saw the overtime as unjust because of the nature of her particular job, and felt pressured by her responsibilities. Added to this, perhaps even because of it, her marriage was showing definite signs of strain. She and Andy never seemed to have time for each other these days. By the time she got in tonight he would have already had his meal and be on his way out to the squash club where he went three times a week. Afterwards she knew he'd stay on and socialise with his friends. "What's the point of the healthy exercise if you undo the good with all that beer afterwards?" she mused. By the time Andy came in she would be in bed, perhaps even asleep.

"Another day gone and we will have hardly spoken a word to each other," she sighed. When weekends came they were so unused to doing things together and even talking to each other that they each went their own way. Trisha had the housework and the shopping, and Andy went to the football match. They were living separate lives in the same house. "Would it have been different if we'd started a family?" she wondered.

The start of the headache was a familiar part of the scenario, and sometimes she would get angry and tearful, going home after work with little appetite for an evening meal, and no energy left to face up to what was wrong with her marriage. Andy wasn't there so there was no opportunity to talk to him anyway.

What she did do was talk to her colleagues at work, and moan about the injustices of her job. She lacked the courage or the skill to discuss the situation openly with her manager, so she became sulky and unhelpful with him, expecting him to be aware of how she felt. None of which solved any of her problems. She also got through huge quantities of headache tablets.

There seemed to be no opportunity to get off the relentless treadmill on which she was running. She could see other people getting on with their lives, even enjoying their jobs, but here she was, day after day, same old routine, nothing to look forward to except her pension when she retired. "If I live that long," she thought.

This is a typical pattern of stress spiralling out of control. This spiral has a sequence of events and has been called the stressor-response chain. The earlier you recognise this sequence the easier it will be to prevent the end result. When the physical and psychological processes are being triggered you need to take action to switch off the response, or at least minimise its effects. The chain is made up of five stages.

Diagram 8

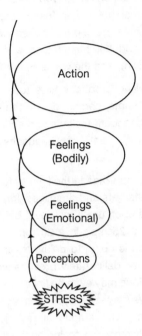

1. The Stressor (the stress itself). What was it that actually happened? What was the stress? What was there about it that caused the stress? In Trisha's case the stressor was the need to work overtime to meet imposed targets.

2. The Perception. The stressor is followed by an interpretation. How was the event understood? How did you see it? What was it is meaning? What was it that you said to yourself when you became aware of the stressor? In Trisha's situation she saw herself as being treated unfairly. As she was already stressed in other parts of her life she probably got her perceptions out of proportion and may even have interpreted it as a deliberate meanness on the part of her manager.

3. Emotions. Depending on the interpretation we put on the stressor there is an emotional response. What are the feelings that come to awareness? What emotions do I sense? As a result of the way she saw the situation Trisha found that she became angry and tearful, and was aware of her frustration.

4. Physical feelings. You next become aware of bodily changes as the emotions trigger the flight/fight/freeze reaction. For Trisha this was headache and loss of appetite, added to an already altered mood. She probably had other reactions as well which were not in immediate consciousness such as a surge in her blood sugar, her heart beating faster, breathing becoming shallower, even raised blood pressure.

5. Actions. Finally there are the actions: how you behave, and the result. Are you now more stressed, or less stressed, than before? In Trisha's case she turned her anger inwards (became tearful), took it out on other people (her colleagues), and allowed it to affect her relationship with her manager and her husband in a negative way. Her chances of promotion began to look pretty slim, and the whole of her life was being affected.

There is an aspect of self-fulfilling prophecy here too. Whenever Trisha had to work overtime she would have the same perception of the situation, and consciously or unconsciously anticipate the subsequent feelings and actions. "Oh, no, the contracts are piling up, I'll have to work overtime, again!". Her headache began at that moment, and the end result was predictable.

It is interesting to view so-called road rage in the light of the stressor-response chain. We are in a hurry, maybe working to targets and deadlines, lots to do and so little time to do it in. Other people make demands upon us. Time spent behind drivers who hog the middle lane of the motorway, or drive at 25 mph in a 30 mph zone, are major stressors. We perceive this as something which is going to delay us, and our perceptions are that the other driver is stupid, a bad driver, deliberately provocative and definitely not as good a driver as ourselves. Our perceptions may even be linked to the type of car they are driving, or the type of person they are. We may stereotype them as an "old woman", a "boy-racer", a "man in a hat", for example. Our emotional response is impatience, anger, and frustration. We become physically tense, switching on the flight/fight response in which the higher brain ceases to function with its usual clarity and our actions then become impulsive, irrational and often completely out of character. There is something too about the impersonal nature of being a car driver. The other drivers cannot clearly see who we are, and we do not know who they are, which seems to give us permission to act differently from the way we would normally behave. It is as if we were wearing a mask, and it is at this point that drivers shake fists at each other and hurl abuse. I once watched a driver get out of his car at traffic lights and attempt to drag the other driver out of his vehicle.

How does stress develop for you? You may not have been aware of the above process and this might be a useful time to help you to analyse what it is that you do and I have given you some space overleaf to write down the factors which cause you stress.

The brain works best with about seven pieces of information at any one time. More than nine and it feels overloaded, less than five and there is not enough challenge. So if there are lots of stresses in your life just now, try to put them under seven broad headings. For example everything connected with the nature of your job, e.g. workload, could come under one heading; management issues, e.g. poor supervision, under another heading; family stressors, e.g. illness, under another one, and so on.

Causes of my stress:

1. ....

2. ....

3. ....

4. ....

5. ....

6. ....

7. ....

Now, I expect you would like space to add more detail, so take seven pieces of paper and write one of these headings across the top of each. Next list the factors causing stress under each of the broad headings, and again try to group these under seven to nine items.

Factors relating to your job might now be listed as lack of career opportunities, financial constraints, working in an open plan office, not having a secretary and so on. You might want to carry on making even more detailed lists to help you identify your stressors in more detail. This will certainly be a useful exercise later on when you are discovering the different ways in which you can handle your stress.

You could now take one aspect of your stress and examine it in the light of the stressor-response chain, applying the following questions to that situation to discover what you would need to do differently to prevent a stressed action response.

Stress busting questions

Stage 1. "What can I do to prevent or change the stress itself?"

You know that certain situations always trigger a stress response in you. Look at the situation. Is it preventable and, if so, how? In what ways might you have even set yourself up for this stress? Could you be more organised yourself? Could you have started the task earlier, or refused to take it on? If you cannot prevent the stress could you at least change part of it to head it off, or reduce the level of stress generated?

Stage 2. Perceptions. "Can I change the way I see it?"

The situations which cause stress are different for each individual, depending on his or her perceptions of the situation. How could you change your perceptions of the stress? One person's stress is another person's challenge, even enjoyment (take parachute jumping!) What is it that you say to yourself when you become aware of this situation? Are you aware of your internal dialogue?

Stage 3. Emotional response. "Can I prevent my emotional response?"

What is the emotional response you become aware of? What are your feelings: anger, depression, dread, guilt, feelings of inadequacy? Try to give your emotion a name.

Stage 4. Bodily feelings. "Can I change the way I handle it by reducing my physical response?"

Could you use stress-busting techniques to keep you calmer and more clear-headed? Could you slow down and make sure that you do not switch on a headache, indigestion, or an irrational action response? Do you need to be more stress-proof, physically, by taking more exercise, or improving your diet and your eating habits?

Stage 5. Action. "Is there a better way to deal with the situation?"

Worrying about it will not make any difference, only action can do that. If the way you are currently handling your stress is not making a difference, what could you do that was more effective? If the level of your current ability does not allow you to handle your stress differently, how do you need to change in order to do that? Do you need to develop your skills (e.g. computer training or develop your management skills)? Do you need to develop your communication ability (e.g. become more assertive, learn how to say no)? Do you need to become better organised (e.g. practise better time management)?

Another strategy for handling stress well is the ability to bounce back like the weeble or kelly doll that always finds its balance. How resilient are you able to be? When stress hits you, can you use a quick coping strategy and get back on your feet again? Is your sense of humour intact? Do you have a good support structure of relationships and friends? Do you make use of opportunities such as queues and waiting times to practice stress-busting techniques and switch off the stress response? Do you have enjoyable leisure pursuits to help you have a fuller life, rather than putting all your energies into your job, for example?

Finally you could ask yourself, "If I cannot change it, avoid it, or handle it differently, do I need to get away from it?" This is the ultimate in removing stress but as you will see in Chapter 10, this should be viewed as a last resort. There are many other things you can do to improve your ability to cope with stress.

It is likely that you have certain ways of behaving under stress and using these questions will help you develop better coping strategies. Albert Einstein once wrote, "The significant problems we face cannot be solved at the same level of thinking we were at when we created them." Stress challenges us to take a mental helicopter to a point above the situation so that we can get a different view on it, and be prepared to entertain new thoughts, new ideas, develop a new focus and a new perspective. Unless we are prepared to think differently, we will not experience any difference. Thought is creative.[1]

The chances are that many of your present behaviours are not useful, having been generated under stress when your rational brain was not fully functioning. Instinctive, irrational behaviour can become the norm under stress.

The difference between effective coping and ineffective coping needs to be looked at in more detail. Many people when they are stressed find themselves involved in displacement activity, which in non-jargon terms means doing anything else at all except the very thing they should be doing. They tidy their desks, remember people they need to phone, and find jobs to do which have been waiting for weeks and suddenly become urgent. All of this might be useful activity, but none of it is what they should be doing at that moment, and in fact they are putting off what they really should be getting on with.

Others find they become obsessed with certain tasks, like a manager friend of mine who, whenever she has a heavy workload, at the very point when she should be ensuring she has some extra leisure time, will insist on clearing out cupboards and cleaning the oven. Things which she has been happily able to ignore when she was more relaxed, suddenly become urgent and demanding.

The only really useful displacement activity is making lists of all the things that you have to do. You should then prioritise the list; decide what you are going to do and when. Next do any preparation work which is needed and then get on and do the tasks, more efficiently and in a way that uses the minimum amount of time.

Displacement activity is a form of maladaptive behaviour. Maladaptive behaviour aims at removing the stressful situation (e.g. by putting it off) but only succeeds in doing this temporarily. It does not deal with the feelings of anxiety nor does it help you be better equipped for future problems. You are not doing yourself any favours either by using ineffective ways of coping with stress. You are likely to be adversely affecting your immune system and your general health. Maladaptive behaviour can also include denial that a problem exists, or poor coping measures such as excessive drinking, increased smoking and use of other "props" such as pills and chocolate.

Remember, if you always do what you have always done, you will always get what you have always got! So if you want to do something about your stress and reduce your stress level, you need to develop new and improved ways of handling it.

But the good news is that research has shown that it is not the major stresses which result in physical or mental breakdown in individuals. It is the accumulation of daily hassles. Human beings have been shown to be able to cope with major life events such as reorganisation at work, personal tragedies, etc. Somehow we find the ability. But it is the daily irritations which may be the most serious triggers of stress. These are ongoing and may never be resolved. They are the constant 'drips' which we have to contend with, and the accumulation of these can be more damaging in the long run than major life events. Perhaps because we trigger our coping mechanisms less readily for minor problems.

It is as important, therefore, that we try to identify the daily hassles and irritations that get us down, and what we might do to prevent them, as it is to identify the major sources of stress. On its own any one of these hassles is very minor and we believe we ought to be able to cope. We do not recognise the build-up, or stop to add them all up, not appreciating that it is one of these minor irritations which could be the straw that breaks the camel's back.

Wendy

Wendy is a teacher. She is also the mother of two school-age children. Every morning her life began in the same way: rush, rush, rush as she kissed her husband goodbye, got the children ready for school, fixed their breakfast, attended to all their last minute requests. "I need a lemon for cookery today!" for example. Finally she bundled them into the car and drove two miles out of her way to drop them off at school, hurrying them into school saying, "Hurry up, I've got a job to go to!". She then faced the rush hour traffic and drove to her own place of work, cursing every red light and traffic tailback. By the time she arrived at work she felt like a chewed piece of string. She had had no breakfast herself and her adrenaline was already flowing freely meaning that the resources she had for her own very demanding job were being used up and the working day had not even begun. Not only that, she was raising two children who were beginning to be stressed themselves because of the hurried start to their own day. They were picking up the stress virus from Jean. Jean's stress didn't finish when she got into school either. She had all her lesson material prepared but she would find someone else hogging the photocopier, there were not enough pencils for her class and she had to get more from the stock-room. She would book the video recorder for a lesson and find that someone else had ignored her booking and taken it to use for their lesson. When she finally got her lesson started she would be constantly interrupted by children from other classes coming in with messages for her, with good work to be shown off, and worst of all to borrow her window-pole (there were never enough to go round and it was so irritating having lessons interrupted for such a trivial item!). Then the final straw would be getting into the staff room a little later than most and finding that all the cups had been used up and no one had washed any. At this point Jean usually let fly at anyone who got in her way.

When life gets like this you need an overview of your stress – the helicopter ride. From your helicopter it is easier to devise ways of dealing with those irritating little things which often cause steam to come out of our ears. I am sure reading Jean's story you could give her lots of advice about what she needed to do to resolve some of her hassles, but Jean in the midst of it could not see where things could be different until she took time out to attend a stress management course. When she sorted out some of the minor hassles (getting the children's clothes ready the night before, preparing packed lunches in advance, getting up 15 minutes earlier, tabling an agenda item at the staff meeting about window poles, for example) she began to reduce some of her daily hassles which reduced her stress levels considerably.

The research into daily hassles can be linked to a principle which is often used in business to identify problems needing to be addressed. The principle is known as the 80:20 or Pareto Principle. It was described by Vilfredo Pareto, an Italian economist, who realised that 80% of Italian wealth was owned by 20% of the population, and he hypothesised that most things in life fall into an 80:20 pattern (or in some cases 70:30 or 60:40). Take for example the clothes that you wear. How many of them do you wear on a day-to-day basis? On reflection you probably realise that you wear 20% of them 80% of the time. Do you collect records, tapes or CDs? How many of them do you play regularly? Yes, 20%, and by regularly you probably mean about 80% of the time.

A sample Pareto graph is shown here, illustrating what a typical analysis might look like. In this illustration F and A account for 49% and 31% respectively. If the factor being measured was customer complaints, for example, the company would be able to see that they could reduce 80% of complaints, by focusing on whatever was represented by F and A which are only 20% of the whole.

Diagram 9

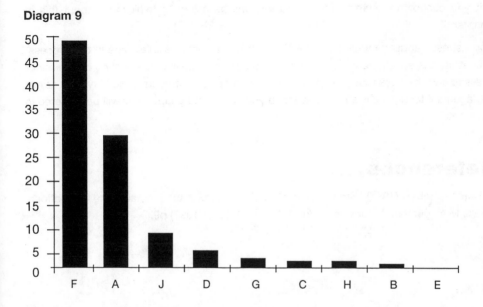

The company does not have to re-engineer the whole product, or retrain all the staff, but merely to concentrate on that important 20%.

Of course you can then go on finding another 20% and another, for as long as you want to do this, but the important point is that you do not have to change everything at once. Changing just 20% will affect the remaining 80%.

I used to find my University teaching stressful at times. Not the teaching itself so much as the minor hassles: walking between classes in separate buildings, carrying all my teaching materials, battling along the corridors. But the greatest stress of all was the photocopying. There just were not enough photocopiers and they were usually out of paper, out of toner, or out of use. Being part-time I relied on being able to get at them when I was in the building, even if I had prepared my material the week before.

A new office manager solved my problems at a stroke. She appointed two of the junior office staff to check the copiers twice a day and ensure they were in working order. This removed 80% of my stress and I made a point of telling her how grateful I was.

This 80:20 principle applies to people too. Managers will discover that 20% of their staff take up 80% of their time. Teachers certainly know that 80% of class disruption is caused by 20% of the pupils, and the police are discovering that 20% of hardened criminals are using up 80% of police time and resources.

So what is your 20%? What do you need to concentrate on to prevent 80% of your daily hassles? Take a moment now to think about this and to check back over your list of stressors. You will not be able to do something about all of your stresses what you are aiming to do is discover the "vital few" that will make the difference. The stresses that you cannot change need to be accepted so that you do not waste energy fighting something that you cannot do anything about and you will be asked to think more about this in Chapter 6.

Good stress handling requires interventions at the earliest possible stage in the process. Your strategies should be worked out when your mind is clear, concentrating on the minor stresses and the 80% that you can do something about. Of course, the very best stress management technique is stress prevention and in the next chapter this will be explored in more detail.

References

1. Holden, Robert (1997) "Stress Busters", in *Stress News*, the journal of the International Stress Management Association. Vol. 9. No. 4 (October 1997) p9.

chapter six

Be your own pilot

During the Second World War American bomber pilots were the subject of a research project on stress. The researchers wanted to understand the stress levels of the pilots and co-pilots, and which of the two was the most stressed. Guess which that was? You're right - the co-pilots! It seemed to indicate that being in control of events, and being a decision maker, reduces the impact of the stress and makes it easier to handle.

Alan

It was Monday morning again. Alan let himself into his office and hung up his coat. As he opened his briefcase and took out the work he'd been doing at the weekend he allowed himself a small smile of satisfaction. Yes, he'd had to work at home again this weekend, but he'd got down to it early on Saturday morning, before the rest of the family had come out of their weekend "slump". Also, because he'd been better prepared than last time, and had chosen a time of day when he was mentally alert, he had got his report finished in record time. Now he would give it to his secretary, whom he could hear arriving in the next office, to proofread and print out, and it would be on Peter's desk by coffee time.

Alan was Personal Assistant to Peter, the Chief Executive of a former public sector organisation which had recently been privatised. There had been a lot of changes recently and the job role of every employee was being evaluated, causing a lot of uncertainty and anxiety. Job descriptions had been re-written and everyone had had to apply for their own job under new contracts and terms of employment. Some staff had been made redundant and others had been moved onto other duties. In the old days staff believed they had a job for life, nowadays no one was so sure. Everyone was under a lot of pressure.

Peter gave Alan quite a lot of responsibility, and as Alan was anxious to prove his worth he was putting in a lot of extra time, usually at the expense of family life. He'd even been known to come in on a Sunday, much to Jean's displeasure. He did wonder whether Peter took as much work home.

Initially, Alan had been worried by all the changes, and found he was sleeping badly and worrying about his job. But more recently he had been learning a thing or two, particularly about stress and how to handle it, and had realised that if he wanted to continue to rise in the organisation he had to demonstrate that he had the ability to do the job, and do it well. So that this week when Peter had employed one of his favourite tactics, which was to throw a file of papers onto Alan's desk with the words "Can you look at that and do me a report on it?", Alan had had his response ready. Usually he would have just agreed to do the work, and then spent the weekend trying to work out what was in Peter's mind. What did he plan to do with the completed report? How long did it need to be? Who was going to read it, and so on? He would often write and re-write the report, even prepare more than one version in case Peter asked for more detail.

On this occasion he was ready. When the request was made Alan's response had been to reach for a notepad and to say to Peter, "OK, could you just fill me in on what you're looking for?" He could tell Peter was a little surprised by this request so he explained, "Are you looking for a detailed report, or a one-page summary, for example? Is it just for your information, or is this to be a briefing paper for several people?" Having got this information from Peter he then went on to check when Peter wanted it, and a little bit more background on the document. Armed with these details Alan then found that actually doing the report only took half of the usual time. There was even opportunity to do some further research during normal working hours, checking on some statistics that he thought were necessary, before taking the report home. He only wished he'd had time to do the whole thing in work time, but at least he'd finished on Saturday by the time Jeremy had to go to football practice, and for the first time in many weeks Alan was able to take him there and stay to watch the play. He could tell Jeremy was pleased, he'd talked non stop in the car on the way to the ground. It was only natural that a nine-year-old should look to his father for encouragement and approval, which on this occasion Alan was able to find time to give. He made a vow that this would happen more often.

Not only that, but feeling so much better about the way he had tackled the work led Alan to feel better about himself, and more relaxed generally. Jeremy wasn't the only one to notice the difference. Jean had been quite surprised when he'd mowed the lawn without needing to be asked, and later, instead of slumping in front of the TV, he had suggested asking her mother to baby-sit and they had gone out for a drink together for the first time in months. Yes, things had definitely started to look up!

There had still been some other work to do which he'd left until Sunday, but he was discovering how to be proactive, to prioritise and plan, and above all to ask questions and get the information before he started on a project. He had also discovered the value of taking regular breaks. There had been several raised eyebrows when he appeared in the canteen at lunch-time, replacing the sandwich at the desk pattern. It enabled him to get back to the office re-charged, having had time for a little creative thought about what he needed to do that afternoon. He found he got through the work quicker too, with fewer mistakes. Yes, he was learning to take control of his stress and prevent it. He was still taking work home but he'd been able to ensure that the time that he did have with his family had been time spent doing things with them rather than just being there - quality time to make up for lack of quantity time. It felt good.

What Alan was doing put him in charge of the situation. He was becoming his own pilot.

In a more recent experiment which looked more closely at the control factor, subjects in a noisy work environment were divided into two groups. One set were given a control button to reduce the amount of background noise when it interfered with productive work. The others were not given a button. Unsurprisingly, the group with the control button were found to be less stressed, and their productivity was unaffected, although not one of them actually used it. Knowing that they could do so, if they wanted, was enough to reduce their stress levels. What this means in stress-management terms is that the more control you have, the less stressed you will be. Taking steps to become more proactive in your life, particularly in relation to those things which cause you stress will reduce the level of perceived stress. There will be many things that you genuinely cannot control, but you can take a long hard look to find out where there might be areas where you could gain more control. Remember the Pareto Principle in Chapter Five? Just look for the important 20%.

Margaret is a business consultant who has to travel huge distances in her work. She tends to find motorway driving very stressful, particularly at busy times of day and at night. Who doesn't? In order to put herself in charge of the situation and reduce the stress, when she is away for several days, she chooses to make the journey late in the evening when the motorways are quiet, arriving very late after a relatively traffic-free journey, or avoids the motorways all together if she has time on her side. She has also made sure that she has the most comfortable car that she can afford and when she last changed cars she bought one with power-assisted steering to take some of the physical stress out of driving. She practises tension-relieving exercises whenever she stops, and when she arrives at her destination. Having a selection of her favourite music cassettes in the car helps her to choose the music she listens to, and for very long journeys she also hires or borrows recorded books, or taped seminars. She swaps these recordings between friends and colleagues, and she told me that her journeys have now become a useful time spent learning about something new instead of frustrating crawls in the traffic.

Are you a pilot, or a co-pilot in your life? Look back at the list you wrote in Chapter Five. Which of these stress factors are within your power to control? How much do you see yourself as a victim of circumstances, and how much power do you believe you have to control events? The greater the degree of power you believe you have the less vulnerable you will be.

Are you anxious about the future? Are you worrying about something that may never happen? Are you wasting energy on negative emotions such as anxiety, fear, boredom and grief. Use your energies for the here and now. The stress that cannot be avoided has to be faced and worked through. As Susan Jeffers' says, the fear, (in this case the stress) will never go away, so you may as well get on and do it. What we need are strategies for handling it more effectively.

Workplace stress is another matter. There are many causes of stress to be found at work, and many strategies which can be employed to put yourself in charge. A firmer, more proactive response is needed. Let us look at some of the workplace problems which might be encountered and some possible solutions. Each of these examples takes the basic source of the stress and suggests an action which will solve it at least temporarily, and perhaps permanently.

If you allow yourself to be given an unrealistic workload the end result will be that your general work performance will deteriorate. It is in your interest and the interest of your employers that you work at your optimum. List everything that you have to do, prioritise the list, then seek a meeting with your manager to discuss these priorities and find out which are the least important items that can be removed from the list. Use a positive approach and have some suggestions to offer which will improve the situation. Do not moan, or complain. Saying, "I'm stressed" may be misunderstood. Say instead, "I've not been able to give as much time to xxx project because of the many priorities I have. Can you help me work out which things are least important and might be left, or delegated to someone else." When new projects are given to you ask your manager to help you decide what you would need to leave, or do to a lower standard as a result. Learn to delegate, and not just individual tasks but whole projects, using these as opportunities to develop more junior staff. This will involve you in training activity, and supervision, but if these are done properly it will mean that you have passed on some of your work permanently to someone else, and increased responsibility could be a strong motivating factor for them. This applies at home too. If workplace pressures are high, consider delegating some home tasks to family members, thus developing an increased sense of responsibility in your children. Hire a cleaner or a gardener. Have someone else do your ironing. The expense will be justified in more family time and improved health leading to longer life.

Through lack of induction training, or because policies have changed, you may be struggling in the dark trying to work out what should be done in particular situations. You may be unaware of company policy or procedure. Do not just guess and hope you have got it right. You could end up with egg on your face, or at the very least be seen to be ineffectual and lose the respect of your colleagues. Be like Alan; ask questions and find out. With the knowledge of what should be done you will work more efficiently. Similarly if you are unclear about your role responsibility, or if your colleagues have unrealistic expectations of your role, a discussion with relevant parties can clarify what is expected of you and relieve your pressure.

A lot of workplace stress comes from poor working relationships with colleagues. When this happens, do not just grin and bear it, try to find out what the problem is and see it from their point of view as well as your own. Do not wait for them to change. If you are the one being affected by the situation take the initiative to improve things. Address the issue directly with the colleague and work something out with them. Use humour and good interpersonal skills to bring about a change. Could a third person help?

Do you believe that your talent is going unrecognised? Has a colleague been promoted over your head? Try to find out why this has happened. Get some feedback in a constructive way from your manager, or the relevant person. Learn from the feedback. Find out what kind of experience or qualifications you lacked. Is it management training you need, or is the problem personality factors? If, having obtained feedback, and acted on it, you still do not get the promotion, find another job. Staying in a job where you are unappreciated is soul destroying and will eat at your self-esteem. Somewhere there is a company who will appreciate your talents, believe this and find them.

Just as you can change your perception of stressful situations, so you can change your perceptions of yourself and your skills and coping abilities. Developing your self-esteem will enhance your feelings of self-control and reduce feelings of helplessness. Avoid giving yourself a hard time, accept yourself as you are, be kind to yourself and reward yourself. Use positive assertion techniques to get feedback from your colleagues and your manager about things you do well.

Are the pressures of the job conflicting with family demands? Try to look at this dispassionately and realistically, then discuss the situation with your manager, and with your family. See if you can to negotiate more family time, perhaps in the shape of less travel, or fewer after-hours meetings. Make sure the time you do spend with your family is quality time and put as much effort into playing as you do into working. Learn to say "No" when appropriate. If you know you have a difficult week coming up, plan ahead with your other commitments, balance the increased work with increasing your relaxation, keep the weekend free. You will do your career a favour, and some of your best ideas will come whilst you are playing, relaxing and having fun.

Make the end of the day when work ends and the rest of your life begins. This is particularly important for those who are self-employed. You might spend a few moments writing down work issues which are on your mind before you leave work and leaving them in a drawer. This is a good time to prepare the "To Do" list for the next day. On your journey home have a regular point on your route where you stop thinking of work problems and start thinking of home. Listen to mood enhancing music as you travel.

Many working environments are unhealthy, physically or psychologically. It is easy to get used to the conditions you work or even live in, and you become inured to the amount of stress they are causing. Check noise levels, cleanliness and hygiene, and pollution levels. Consider the effect that artificial lighting and air conditioning may be having and make an effort to get some natural light and fresh air in the middle of the day. Always wear ear defenders, masks, gloves, or whatever other safety equipment the company may provide for your job, and if they have not been provided get them. The Health and Safety Executive will provide help if needed.

You are not your job. Do not let your job define who you are. You job is just something you do to earn money to live. If you become too closely identified with your job and it goes through serious pressure, redundancy or reorganisation perhaps, you and your self-esteem go with it. Keeping your nose to the grindstone is no way to live. Take yourself and your work less seriously. Develop your sense of humour. Do not measure your status by how much you earn, or how busy you are. Life is more than a pay cheque.

Becoming proactive in the ways suggested here will help you deal with the immediate problem, and it will give you a sense of achievement, and develop your confidence in dealing with similar situations in the future.

Another area where this control factor is important is change, whether in our personal or our work lives. Change has been found to be one of the most significant factors in the cause of stress today. Abraham Lincoln said the only two certainties in life were death and taxes. I would add another one to that list for the present age, and that would be change. Change has become an inevitable aspect of life as technology, society, working practices, in fact every part of our lives are subject to continuous evolution. It is no good facing each change, as many do, with the philosophy, "Well, it will be all right when we get this present re-organisation over with and get back to normal". People who do this are in for a shock. There never will be a normal again, and that kind of grin and bear it but do not get involved attitude can make change even more stressful. Change is not just a one-off re-organisation, it is continuous and rapid.

When the changes are those that we have instigated ourselves, we have a high degree of control and, whilst the changes may be stressful, somehow we cope. Moving house, for example, is said to be one of the most stressful experiences after divorce and bereavement. But many of us choose to subject ourselves to this stress because we want to live in a larger house, or a different neighbourhood. If we are forced to move house, however, perhaps because of job changes, or after divorce, this is not entirely our choice. This may be an imposed change, and therefore the degree of stress is much higher.

Many workplace changes are those over which we have little control, company re-organisation and response to government directives for example. If we do not perceive that we have any control over even a part of the change, stress levels are found to be much higher. Because change is so much a part of today's work environment, the skills for handling it are vital for today's generation, and learning these are important as part of stress prevention.

How can we survive change? How can we ensure that we handle the stresses associated with change and still remain healthy, well-balanced individuals with nourishing relationships? The first step is to decide where we want to direct our energies. It is all too easy to waste time and energy attempting to prevent or to sabotage changes which are inevitable. At the same time we may be missing opportunities presented by the situation, and failing to realise that there are some aspects of it which might be within our control.

When we stop complaining about, and wasting negative energy on, things which cannot be changed we have the ability to develop a new perspective and find out what advantages there may be for us in the current situation. This also gives the opportunity to discover the WIFM in the situation. WIFM stands for What's In It For Me?, and is about appreciating that within every problem there is an opportunity. For example you may be being asked to give up your day off because of staff shortages, but the WIFM might be that you are then in a stronger negotiating position and can choose your next day off, arranging it at a more favourable time to yourself.

You may like to use the following advice which is given by Ursula Markham[2]. "If you are faced with a change which is causing you some anxiety take a little time to list the different aspects of the problem and reduce it to manageable chunks. Somehow seeing things in black and white can make them more manageable than when they are just worries and fears running around in our heads. Also doing something, however small, can bring a sense of achievement and reduce the worry as you realise that you do have a degree of control, particularly over your own reactions."

1. What is the problem?

_____

_____

2. What aspects can I do nothing about?

_____

_____

3. What are the benefits, however trivial, of the current situation?

_____

_____

4. What are my greatest fears?

_____

_____

5. What can I do about each?

_____

_____

Another thing you can do when faced with a stressful situation brought about by an unwanted change in your life is draw up a balance sheet indicating both the positive and negative long-term aspects of this change. But do not try to do all this in one day. On good days you will have lots of positive ideas to write down, on bad days you probably will not be able to think of a single positive thing. So do it over several days, good and bad, and you are most likely to get a realistic summary.

It is also true that change is not necessarily all good. Sometimes we feel moved to oppose some changes, ethically, and stand up for important values which might be endangered. The challenge in this situation is to differentiate between resisting changes just because we would prefer to cling to the old ways, or because we see something good being swept away, or because we really do not believe the new ways will result in significant improvements.

Remember this prayer?

> *"God*
> *grant me the Serenity to accept the things*
> *I cannot change...*
> *Courage to change the things I can*
> *and Wisdom to know the difference."*

What we need in the midst of change is this wisdom to know the difference. C Stephen Lynn, Chief Executive Officer of Shoneys' Inc. in America[3], says of the way he handles stress, "I never lose my spiritual perspective. My job is to run the race well. God chooses who the winners are. If I can recognise what is my responsibility and give up what I do not have authority over, it takes off an awful lot of stress".

Denis Waitley[4] tells the story about a native tribe in South America whom scientists studied because, for many generations, they have been dying prematurely from a strange illness. It was finally discovered that the disease was caused by the bite of an insect, which lives in the walls of their homes. The natives have several possible solutions: they can destroy the insect with an insecticide; they can destroy and rebuild their homes; they can move to another area where there are no such insects; or they can continue to live and die early, just as they have done for generations. They have chosen to remain as they are and die early, taking the path of least resistance and no change.

This highlights another attitude which we might have towards change and feeling comfortable with what we have. Generally humans are creatures of habit and find security in familiar routines, even when the routines are time-consuming and inefficient, or life-threatening, as in the above example. We also see this in people's refusal to give up smoking or change to a healthy diet or lifestyle. Are you resisting opportunities to reduce your stress because it would mean changing some old habit, or giving up some familiar routine?

People like to have as much control as possible and the familiar allows us to exercise this, particularly at work. In our private lives we generally have more decision-making ability, but at work it is often the reverse. When a change is imposed we may feel a sense of powerlessness and lack of control which can trigger uncertainty and apprehension.

If your organisation is undergoing change (and which one isn't?) there is particular need for you to learn to be proactive and look for the advantages. Special skills are needed since too much change, handled badly, can move us towards burnout. This is because we are using up our adaptation energy in order to learn new skills and new policies, and adapt to new work procedures, not to mention new management and work colleagues. Alan's organisation had been forced to make a lot of changes due to the privatisation and many of the staff were finding these very difficult. Some people welcomed the changes, seeing them as much needed opportunities to streamline the organisation and help it become more efficient. Many hated it, and there were others who were actively resisting and even sabotaging the changes. If we have insufficient information about the changes, we worry about what will happen, and how we will cope with the differences. We may fear failure, worry about looking stupid, about loss of responsibility or status. Have our previous skills become obsolete? Do we have the ability to learn new skills and become as competent as we are now? If someone new is taking over, will they respect the contributions we have made in the past and will they be as good as the previous manager to whom we gave our loyalty?

We need to think very hard about why we are resisting change and try to see it as a challenge rather than a threat. You will find a Change Questionnaire in Appendix (ii) which will help you to assess your own attitudes to change. Perhaps, like Alan, you could use the change to evaluate your present job and consider new ways of doing familiar tasks it could well be an opportunity to develop new skills and shift direction.

I am saddened when I talk to people who are facing change within their organisations and yet refuse to face up to its inevitability. They may have been working for the same organisation for years and the company is about to undergo massive reorganisation, perhaps due to a takeover or change in markets. Many people are like frightened rabbits, frozen in the headlights of an oncoming car. They are terrified that they are about to become casualties and yet hope against hope that they will somehow escape.

Just as organisations need to be one step ahead of their competitors if they are to survive in today's market place, so too do their employees. We need to look ahead to changes that are likely to happen, and begin to look for the opportunities in them, the WIFM. That helicopter is useful again here. When you are not emotionally involved and can take a more distant view of a situation, it is possible to be aware of what is likely to happen and to prepare for the changes in a positive way.

Learn to be your own pilot and make decisions which will reduce your stress levels. Put yourself in charge. The next chapter will help you to understand some of the ways in which you can change your perceptions by understanding what is happening in your brain.

References

1. Jeffers, Susan (1987) *Feel the Fear and Do It Anyway*, Arrow Books, Century Hutchinson, London.

2. Markham, Ursula (1993) *Living With Change*, Element Books, Shaftesbury, Dorset.

3. Lynn, Syephen (in *Forbes*, June 2, 1997 v159 n11 p20(2))

4. Waitley, Denis (1986) *The Winner's Edge*, Berkley Books.

chapter seven

Chained to the last seat of the bus - directing your brain

The earlier in the stressor-response chain you can intervene, the more successful you will be in heading off stress. The first stage in the chain is your perceptions. If you can learn to appreciate what your perceptions of a situation are, how you are seeing those things which cause you stress, you then have the choice to change your view of them and change the way you behave.

Richard Bandler[1] said, "I want you to find out how you can learn to change your own experience, and get some control over what happens in your brain. Most people are prisoners of their own brains. It is as if they are chained to the last seat of the bus and someone else is driving. I want you to learn how to drive your own bus. If you do not give your brain a little direction, either it will just run randomly on its own, or other people will find ways to run it for you and they may not always have your best interests in mind. Even if they do, they may get it wrong!"

Does that sound like you?

I slowed my car to a halt behind the queue of traffic on the dual carriageway ahead. 'Damn, a traffic jam!' I muttered. 'The very thing I could do without.' As I braked I heard the announcer on the car radio issue a warning to traffic about bridge repair works causing a three-mile tailback. I groaned inwardly realising that he was talking about the road that I was on at that moment. I looked despairingly ahead for an opportunity to turn off, but there was no comforting sign to be seen, and in any case the traffic was moving so slowly it wouldn't help much.

The infuriating thing was that I needn't have been here at all. I was on my way to another town, and had taken the wrong turn from the motorway four miles earlier, in a moment's inattention. Without the bridge repair works that wouldn't have been an enormous problem. I could have used this route and still arrived in good time for the seminar which I was to conduct that day for staff at the hospital.

Once upon a time my reaction would have been to panic. I was a self-employed training consultant and could not afford to be late for a seminar. This was my first assignment at this hospital and my livelihood depended on customers booking further seminars with me. I pride myself on my high standards and being in plenty of time for each seminar is obviously important. Before each seminar I make sure the room is set up, and all equipment working. I unpack my teaching materials and handouts and then spend some time making sure that I mentally prepared for the day's training. Today I knew I would be lucky to arrive on time, and with every moment spent in this traffic I began to fear that I would, in fact, be late. My heart began to sink.

The interesting thing was that today I was going to be talking about Restoring Personal Energy and one of the main points was the understanding of how one's mental attitude could result in negative or positive energy which would, in turn, affect performance. This is the critical difference between success and failure. I became only too aware that the quality of my own reaction at this time would make an enormous difference to my state of mind on arrival. If I allowed a state of high negative energy to develop, this would be characterised by frustration, and anger, resulting in tension and stress. In turn this would affect my state of mind and my ability to think clearly and logically about my teaching material. It would also affect how I put my ideas across and my interaction with the delegates.

Today would be the first time I had taught this particular subject. I had developed it at the request of the Nurse Teacher who recognised how stressed and de-motivated many of the nurses were becoming as a result of high work loads and diminishing resources. Teaching a new subject in itself was causing some apprehension.

To make matters worse, every time I reached for my mobile phone and diary, to find and dial the number of the hospital, the traffic began to move and I had to put it down again. By the time I finally got through there was only an answering machine to take my message they were obviously already on their way to the staff training centre, and here I was with at least another half hour's journey once the traffic cleared.

"OK', I thought to myself, "I can't get out of this situation, and there is nothing I can do about it now. What is the worst thing that could happen?"

I ran all the possible scenarios through my mind. I created a disastrous picture of arriving at the hospital, to find the delegates all in their seats, and myself arriving, flustered, and stressed, to teach a seminar about the relationship between mental state and high performance.

"Not a good illustration", I acknowledged. "So, what do I need to do to change. What I can do is first take control of my mind and my emotions. In that way when I do arrive I can start straight in to my presentation, in a convincing way. Secondly, even if I am late, I will need to see this as a challenge, be calm and unflustered, and think clearly and logically."

So, as I stopped and started in the traffic, instead of fuming inwardly at the delay as I might have done before, I remembered the principles which I was now on my way to teach. I remained calm, practised deep breathing to control the tension, and began to rehearse, mentally, the first section of my presentation.

Eventually the traffic began to move, but instead of speeding off in the direction of the hospital, I took time to pull in to the side of the road and consult the map in order to choose the best route to my destination so that I wouldn't be delayed further.

When I finally arrived the staff had all assembled and it was already fifteen minutes after my advertised starting time. I did of course apologise, and explain. But instead of being flustered and panicking I was able to take my place at the front of the room immediately, introduce myself and lose no time in beginning my presentation. Because I had been able to think clearly whilst still in my car, and work out the best way to handle the situation if I was late, I had made a plan to divide the delegates into small groups for a discussion exercise at an early stage in the proceedings and this I did. Whilst they were involved in this activity, I had time to unpack my learning materials, and check the overhead projector, and when they reconvened I was able to carry on as planned. Not only that, but at an appropriate stage in the seminar I was able to refer back to my own experience that morning to illustrate to my delegates the point I was making about high negative energy, showing how by keeping the energy positive I had been able to think more clearly and resourcefully.

That seminar is one of the best I have conducted and I am now invited back regularly to run that particular seminar for the hospital staff.

We often set ourselves limits and put negative connotations onto life events, not realising that these very limits are what hold us back and take away our personal power. Just like Bridget, a colleague of mine in Health Service days, who wanted to set up her own business and came to discuss this with me. She outlined her ideas and described how she thought they could work, becoming very enthusiastic about them. Then she said to me, "But, I am no good at selling. I couldn't market myself." My eyebrows shot up and I was able to show Bridget that for the last half hour she had been doing exactly that. She had been selling herself and her ideas to me without realising what she was doing. She had limited herself by a belief that she did not have that skill and therefore was not capable of developing it. Her internal belief was, "I'd be no good at selling" which was based on past experience.

I am sure she often thought back to that conversation over the years she spent setting up and developing a successful business, watching it grow from year to year. It was a process which she would have been unable to undertake without the self-marketing skills which she once believed she did not have.

Our inner dialogue and internal messages are responsible for our perceptions and this, which can be described as the internal chatterbox, can unconsciously control our lives. Noam Chomsky[2], the linguist, says that there are in fact two levels to this dialogue. He calls these levels the surface structure, which is everything we say to ourselves and to other people, and the deep structure, which is the information going around in our heads of which we are not consciously aware, and do not consciously express.

You are probably aware of the surface structure of your "chatterbox". With awareness some of your deep structure can become more conscious and when it does it loses some of its power over your behaviour. It no longer has the power to control the way you act, just as my awareness of my negative emotions enabled me to take control and change my reactions to the traffic jam. The things we say to ourselves result from the way in which we view an event when it happens, rather than from the stress itself.

Your life events do not need to be the determining factor in your life if you change the way you see them, you can change your reactions and change your life. Some early research into stress seemed to indicate that stress was caused by a culmination of life events - such as divorce, bereavement, illness, financial difficulties. (See Appendix iii). More recent research puts another perspective on this, emphasising that it is not what happens to you that is the stressor, it is what you do with what happens to you; your reactions and your subsequent actions.

We generally believe that the way in which we perceive a situation must be a true representation of events. We then act according to our perceptions or interpretations of the events or the communications from others. But our interpretations of these are not always correct. Our perceptions can play tricks on us. Have you ever asked someone to do something and then they did the exact opposite, saying, "But, I thought you meant..." Take the famous picture below and the expressions overleaf. If you have not seen it before take a moment or two to look at the picture which is a copy of W.E. Hill's drawing for Puck[3]. What do you see?

Diagram 10. Old/Young Woman

Most people when they first see the picture see an old woman, her head covered in a shawl, her chin sunk deep in her fur coat. As you continue to gaze at the picture your perception changes, and you see a young woman, facing away from you. The old woman's mouth is now the young woman's necklace, the old woman's eye is the young woman's ear, and so on.

Diagram 11. Perceptions

The expressions actually read "Paris in the the spring", "A bird in the the hand", and "Once in a a lifetime". Your previous experience affected your expectation here, and you saw what you thought you were going to see. This is an example of how we often distort what we read and what we hear to fit in with our expectations. These simple illustrations demonstrate the sort of processes that occur in our thinking. We delete, we distort and we generalise information so that it becomes translated into what we think we should see and hear.

Armed with this realisation you can ask yourself some simple questions about the things which cause you stress which will make you much more powerful in dealing with them, and help reduce the stress generated from, or helped along by, the chatterbox. For example ask yourself these simple questions: "How did I interpret this event?" "What was its meaning to me?" "What did I say to myself when this happened?"

This, of course, is part of the second link in the stressor-response chain. What you say to yourself and believe about the stress will determine the quality of your emotions and your subsequent reactions.

Some examples of statements which could lead to feelings of stress are "Uh, uh, here comes the boss again, he doesn't look very pleased, what have I done wrong?". Or, "They won't want me in this job, I am too old." Or, "You stupid woman, why did you do that? You always jump in with both feet first, why did not you think it out more carefully?"

Of course, the quality of the dialogue then affects our subsequent actions and eventually our feelings. For example if you say to yourself, "Oh, here comes the boss, he's frowning and looking abstracted. I wonder what he's got on his mind?". It may well be that the boss's expression has nothing to do with you and if you keep an open mind you are not setting yourself up for stress. Or, "Because I am an older person I have a lot of wisdom and maturity to bring to this job. I must make sure they realise this." Or, "That was a stupid thing to do, but it doesn't mean I am a stupid person. Next time I will remember to wait a moment or two before jumping in."

What do you say to yourself in situations of stress? Look back at your stress sources which you listed in Chapter Five and see if you can identify what you habitually say to yourself about each of these situations. How might you change that dialogue? How might you re-frame it? Make a note of some of them here.

Remember there is always more than one way to view a situation, and the more ways you

Situation	Unhelpful self-talk or negative thoughts	Positive rational alternative

have, the more control you have over the way you will react. This is called re-framing. When we re-frame a situation we become our own film director or in this case our own life director. Just imagine that you have control of a very powerful camera which can zoom in and zoom out from any situation. It can see the fine details and also the big picture. You can direct in full colour, or in black and white. You can view the situation as a panorama or put a frame around it like one of those artistic shots seen through an archway, or framed by the branch of a tree. You can include a detail such as a figure to emphasise perspective, or you can use trick shots to make things appear bigger or smaller than they are. In a similar way you can control and direct your thoughts, looking at the big picture or examining the fine detail, or looking at a situation from someone's else perspective, or imagining how it could be different.

The examples I gave earlier are ways of re-framing. What are the situations that are

Situation I could re-frame	Way in I could re-frame it

causing you pain and stress? Go back to your earlier examples and list here the ones that you might be able to re-frame, and the way in which you could do that.

Still stuck? Have a look at the problem solving questions on the next page, they may give you some ideas for changing your perspectives. The exact words you use are also very powerful in translating your thoughts into feelings. A word such as angry contains much more emotion than the word cross for example. An understanding of how the words you use can help change the emotion, and thus the degree of stress resulting, will increase your degree of control.

In his book *Awaken the Giant Within*, Anthony Robbins[4] says, "Simply by changing your habitual vocabulary - the words you consistently use to describe the emotions of your life you can instantaneously change how you think, how you feel, and how you live."

He reminds us of the power of words and how Winston Churchill used this power, sending "the English language into battle". Churchill's famous call to his people to make this their finest hour resulted in tremendous courage being demonstrated, and crushed Hitler's belief about the invincibility of his war machine.

Robbins also says, "Many of us are aware of the powerful part words have played in our history, of the power that great speakers have to move us, but few of us are aware of our own power to use these same words to move ourselves emotionally, to challenge, to embolden, and strengthen our spirits, to move ourselves to action, to seek greater richness from this gift we call life."

Choosing and using the right words to describe our situation, and our emotions, is a key to changing the way we feel and the way we act in a situation. Advertisers are only too aware of the importance of words in persuading us of the value, usefulness and desirability of a product. We too can make use of their importance.

If the words you are using are creating a state that disempowers you, that cause you to feel and act in ways that block your achievement, get rid of those words and replace them with those that empower you. Using a new word can cause you to break your emotional pattern, and everything can change. Try it! There are some examples on the next page for you to play around with.

Negative Emotion/Expression	Transforms into
I am feeling	*I am feeling*
angry	cross
afraid	apprehensive
anxious	concerned
confused	unclear
depressed	a bit down
destroyed	set back
disgusted	surprised
full of dread	challenged
embarrassed	stimulated
exhausted	tired

What are some of your favourite words? Notice from this point onwards what words you habitually use when you are in a negative emotional state. Similarly you might want to use a stronger word to increase the power of your emotion when you feel that you are in danger of being ignored or put down. You do not have to start throwing things around or stamping your feet, but when you feel angry about something it might be appropriate to simply say, "I feel very angry about that", or even "I feel furious".

Be aware also of the importance of using the word "I" to own those emotions. Do not ever fall into the trap of saying: "You make me angry", for example. With the "you" statement you put the other person in a position of power, knowing exactly what to do every time they want to make you angry. They are your feelings, they happen inside you, in ways of which you may not be consciously aware yet, so own them, and be responsible for them. Instead, try saying, "I feel angry when you do that". They are similar words, but have a different meaning. You can then begin to try to find out just how you create those angry feelings in that situation.

When you find yourself saying, "I can't....", try changing it to "I have not been able to.... before". Remember if a human being can do it, then there is no reason why you cannot - if you want to. The word cannot (and we are told there is no such word anyway) closes the door on our experience, whereas changing the way you make the statement opens the door to the possibility of change.

People who have given up smoking report that the significant change happens when they no longer say, "I am trying to give up smoking" but can say, "I am a non-smoker". The actual form of the words is what makes the difference.

Pat, who attended some of my assertiveness classes was trying to improve her self-esteem. She told me that on the telephone she usually announced herself by saying, "Nuisance here", and similarly she described her rather difficult daughter as "Madam". These labels affected the way in which she viewed herself and her daughter and blocked the possibility of change.

In the space below you could begin to think of those disempowering words which you habitually use, and as you think of them discover a more empowering word you could use in its place.

Try three examples.

Old Word	to	New Word
....	to	....
....	to	....
....	to	....

Exactly the same thing happens with pleasant experiences. We lower the intensity of our feelings about them by using words which somehow reduce them. We use words like, "Okay, all right, nice, comfortable, fine, fair." Here are some examples of words which would allow you to increase the intensity of good feelings in a similar way. You could also add to those with some words of your own.

Good Word	Great Word
From	**To**
I'm feeling	*I'm feeling*
alert	energised
all right	great
awake	raring to go
comfortable	smashing
curious	fascinated
determined	unstoppable
good	tremendous
fine	awesome
good	wonderful
nice	superb

Now try out some of your old words and see how you might be able to change them.

Old Word   to   **New Word**

....   to   ....

....   to   ....

....   to   ....

When Norman Vincent Peale[5] first wrote *The Power of Positive Thinking* many years ago (I was in my teens), it had a popular appeal but then disappeared from book shops for a long time. It has enjoyed a recent revival and it has now been reprinted many times. Why? I believe that when it was written it was a bit ahead of its time. People didn't understand how positive thinking works and saw it as "trying to kid yourself" - some sort of panacea. Since then a lot of research has been done and experiments conducted into how the mind works. What is being discovered is that Norman Vincent Peale had some of the right ideas. We programme our minds through our internal dialogue and then we act upon that programme. So it is possible to set yourself up for failure by a negative viewpoint - a self-fulfilling prophecy in fact.

People often believe that positive thinking is waking up in the morning and saying to yourself something like, "Every day, in every way, I'm getting better and better". That isn't positive thinking. Some people might even regard this as trying to fool yourself or tell yourself lies. It doesn't work, because you don't really believe it.

It's not a question of saying, "I am calm and confident when I speak at a meeting," and trying to get yourself to believe it. Instead you could say, "I can learn to be calm and confident when I speak at a meeting". This opens the door to fresh possibilities. True positive thinking is the realisation that for every negative there is a positive, and life is full of possibilities.

Negative thinkers always look for what's missing, whilst positive thinkers look for possibilities and what can be learned from a situation, no matter how black it may seem at the time. Take the picture overleaf. What do you see? Observe carefully before reading on.

Diagram 12. Bottle of Wine

The picture is a bottle of wine, from which some of the contents have been consumed. (I choose my words with care.)

I regularly show this picture to University students, and on one particular occasion a student said to me some time afterwards, "When you showed us that picture and asked us what we saw, I thought, 'any idiot can see it's a half empty bottle of wine!' I was amazed when you pointed out that it was also a half full bottle of wine." She went on to tell me that she hadn't realised that she had power over her own mind. "I thought that was just the way I was," she said. She told me that it had totally transformed her thinking and brought greater power and confidence to her life.

Are you a negative or a positive thinker? What did you see when you first looked at the picture?

Reading Anthony Robbins' book helped me to see how it is possible to consciously turn around a set-back or a negative event so that it doesn't totally destroy you. I had been reading *Awaken the Giant Within* one summer. It was the summer when we were planning to enjoy sailing in a 9 metre catamaran that my husband and I had been "doing up", to take to the Mediterranean and use for our retirement. We had bought her quite cheaply two years previously because she was in a rather neglected condition and needed a lot of tender loving care. After two years working on her we were looking forward to "putting her through her paces". I loved that boat dearly, and we called her *Double Vision*.

We kept her on a mooring and used her most weekends. On one particular weekend we were unable to go, and during that week-end someone got aboard, was able to start the engine and sailed her up to St. Bees in Cumbria, where he left her on a shingle beach. The tide that night was particularly high, and there was a strong wind. The result was that the boat was dashed to pieces on the rocks and shingle by the time daylight came, and the

I spent several sleepless nights and tearful days in the following week, until I came across Tony Robbins' Problem Solving Questions. Robbins says that no matter what we're involved with in our lives we are going to come across problems. These are roadblocks to personal and professional progress. He calls them "gifts" and says that the question is not whether we're going to have problems, but how we're going to deal with them when they come up.

He suggests five questions which he uses for any type of problem, and since using them I have found that they have had great impact on my life and situations which I have needed to face.

Problem Solving Questions

1. What is great about this problem?

2. What is not perfect yet?

3. What am I willing to do to make it the way I want it?

4. What am I willing to no longer do in order to make it the way I want it?

5. How can I enjoy the process while I do what is necessary to make it the way I want it?

I used these questions immediately with regard to my feelings about the boat. I realised that I was wasting energy on negative emotions and that there was absolutely nothing I could do to bring my beloved boat back. So I started to answer the Problem Solving Questions.

1. "What is great about this problem?"

One of the main "greats" for us was the fact that no one was aboard the boat - there was no loss of life or personal injury, and we did have her insured.

2. "What is not yet perfect?"

We had a long list here, the main one being that we no longer owned our beautiful boat.

3. "What am I willing to do to make it the way I want it?"

Our actions here focused around completing the insurance claim to the insurer's satisfaction with the amount of tedious detail they required, and several trips to Cumbria to deal with salvage.

4. "What am I willing to no longer do in order to make it the way I want it?"

We stopped moaning and just got on with what needed to be done.

5. "How can I enjoy the process while I do what is necessary to make it the way I want it?"

This needs to be a way to make it fun. A hard one when you're facing a gloomy situation! But it was summer, and Cumbria is a great part of the world. So, we turned our trips there

But it was summer, and Cumbria is a great part of the world. So, we turned our trips there into summer picnics, even taking friends with us and staying overnight. In this way we turned some of our painful memories into more pleasant ones.

By having these five questions to use on a regular basis I now have a pattern of how to deal with problems that instantly change my focus and give me the resources I need. I have used them again and again, and found them transforming. I used to be quite a moaning kind of person and hated to have to deal with problems. Now I find that although the problem may not go away it's exciting to see what will result from a positive approach.

You too can learn as I have, how to gain some control over what happens in your brain in order to change your experience. Another process which I have found useful is called Thought Stopping which helps you to avoid dwelling on negative and stress-inducing thoughts and memories and it works like this. When you become aware that your thoughts are taking a negative turn, shout "Stop!" in your head. Then firmly switch your mind back to a pleasant subject that you enjoy thinking about, such as a favourite beauty spot and become aware of how your feelings change as you fully remember how you felt when you were in that place. The theory is that the mind cannot deal with two opposing feelings at once, and so the first, negative emotion is defused. At a later date simply thinking of that same pleasant subject will produce the positive feelings.

Changing our perceptions changes our emotions. In the next chapter you will begin to learn how to take more control over your bodily sensations which can change your physiology and lessen tension. Changing our physiology also changes our feelings and so you are learning how to gain more control.

References

1. Bandler, Richard (1985) *Using Your Brain - For A Change.*

2. Chomsky, Noam (1965) *Aspects of the Theory of Syntax*, MIT Press.

3. Napier, Rodney W and Gershenfeld, Matti (1973) "The Old Lady: A Classic Example" in *Groups: Theory and Experience, Instructors Manual*, Houghton Mifflin Co, Boston.

4. Robbins, Anthony, (1992) *Awaken the Giant Within*, Simon and Schuster, London.

5. Peale, Norman Vincent (1996 reprint) *The Power of Positive Thinking*, Fawcett Crest.

chapter eight

Busy doing nothing?

Have you ever noticed how you are, physically, when you are apparently doing nothing? You may be in a queue, waiting for someone or something, or perhaps watching TV, or at the theatre. These are usually times when people say they are feeling relaxed. If that were the case you would expect your body to be at rest, and still. If you were to do a body check you would actually find quite a bit of residual tension as your body continues to respond to what is going on in your mind. Like Derek in the story below you may be going over the events of the day, even whilst watching something on TV.

Derek

The radio crackled and a familiar voice came over the airwaves, "Alpha 642, Apha 642, are you receiving me?" Derek, immediately alert, responded to his call sign and switching on his siren was soon speeding in his ambulance down the dual carriageway following the instructions he had been given, whilst his partner, Frank, in the passenger seat checked the directions. The call was to a road accident at a set of traffic lights. No one was badly injured and, after transporting the driver of one of the vehicles to hospital for a check-up, just in case, they were on their way back to HQ ready for another call. Today had been uneventful so far, and Derek was both glad and sorry. He enjoyed the buzz which his job gave him, and knew that he lived on something of an adrenaline high. As he waited for his instructions for the next job his fingers drummed the wheel impatiently, and he felt the familiar tension across his shoulders. By the time he finished his shift he was often stiff and sore. Some days he was still buzzing when he got home, and it was just as well that his partner was also an ambulance woman, which helped her to understand. They were both off shift together tonight, a rare occasion, and Derek was planning to suggest a meal out because, even though Julie understood, their combined inability to switch off was threatening their relationship and there were times when sharp words led to angry exchanges like the one they had had last night over nothing at all.

Some days Derek prowled around the house, unable to sleep for several hours after coming off shift, knowing he should have something to eat, but unable to face food just yet. His digestive system took a long time to settle down and he often had heart-burn and chest pains after food. He would re-live the events of the day over and over in his mind, asking himself if he had done the right thing, checking with himself the procedures he had used and the action he had taken. He could never quite be satisfied that he had done everything possible, and this was doubly so when the casualty had not pulled through. At these times Julie and he usually avoided each other, knowing that the slightest thing could turn into a major row. It wasn't easy being in the ambulance service.

The radio crackled again and they were on their way to another job. Hearts beating, pulses racing, eager to do the job they had been trained to do, administering assistance to the injured and helping to save lives.

We use up a lot of energy in tension and restless movement. We clench our fists, tap our toes, bite our nails, hunch our shoulders, drum our fingers, and fidget, even when we are supposed to be at rest. We hold our bodies in a tense position as if at any moment we might need to leap up and spring into some kind of action. We really are busy doing nothing. Is there any wonder that we feel tired at the end of the day, and feel exhausted? We may not have had to take part in any physical activity but we allow our bodies to behave as though we have. The result is that the stress response is still switched on as we wait for the signal to act.

What about the mind, too. You may be at rest at the end of the day, but do you take work problems home with you? Do you find yourself worrying about them, even when you are soaking in a nice relaxing bath, or trying to get off to sleep?

Derek noticed this. He discovered that whilst he was sitting in his ambulance waiting to be sent out on a call, and even when he was waiting in the rest room, he was physically keyed up. He clenched his hands, stiffened the small of his back, tapped his toes, hunched his shoulders and thrust his head forwards. He drove like that too, arriving home in the evening tired, bad tempered, irritable, and all he wanted to do was to sleep in front of the TV. He was not very exciting company for his partner. Even when his day had been uneventful, consisting of nothing more than routine journeys backwards and forwards to the hospital, and long periods of waiting in the ambulance station, he was still like this.

After learning to perform a body check, he was able to recognise what he was doing and consciously relax each part of his body which was not in use. He then made the surprising discovery that he was actually more mentally alert when relaxed, and more able to make quick decisions. He saved the physical tension mode for when it was needed and found that at the end of the day he still had some energy left for his partner. You might like to do this for yourself to discover how relaxed you are when you are seemingly at rest.

Stress buster No. 1

How to perform a quick body check[1]:

◆ As you begin... FREEZE. Do not move. Now pay attention to your body sensations and position.

◆ Can you drop your shoulders? If so, your muscles were unnecessarily raising them.

◆ Are your forearm muscles able to relax more? If so you were unnecessarily tensing them.

◆ Is your body seated (or standing) in a position in which you appear ready to do something active? If so your muscles were unnecessarily contracted.

◆ Can your forehead relax more? If so you were tensing those muscles for no useful purpose.

◆ Check your stomach, buttocks, thighs and calf muscles. Are they, too, contracted more than is necessary?

◆ Unnecessary muscle contraction is called bracing. Many of us brace our muscles and suffer tension headaches, neck aches or bad backs as a result.

◆ Take a moment for yourself now ... concentrate on just letting your muscles relax. Notice how that feels.

Now you can know what your body is really doing, and where you hold most of your tension; you are able to do something about it. Waiting in queues need no longer be wasted time, but time that you can use to give yourself a body check and learn to relax as Derek did. Later on in this chapter, I will teach you some specific relaxation techniques that you can use at this time.

Learning to switch off the stress response is absolutely vital in order to return your body to a normal state after stress, and can help you gain control of your feelings during a stressful time. You will remember from an earlier chapter how the body reacts when it receives alarm messages. One of the these reactions is that we begin to breathe incorrectly. Try this experiment - sit on the edge of your chair, and think of something you find rather frightening, and notice how you are breathing. It will probably be fast, emphasising the in breath and making your collar bone rise and fall. If you continue for more than a few seconds you will start to feel tense and perhaps panicky, so stop! Sit back and let your breathing return to normal. People who are tense tend to breathe incorrectly and do this for so long that it begins to feel normal. In order to change, at first you have to feel wrong to be right.

When your heart beats fast, more adrenaline gets released into your blood which makes your heart beat even faster and release even more adrenaline. It is a vicious circle. To conserve this adrenaline you need to get a lot of oxygen into your lungs and that will slow down your heart rate.

So what do you need to do? Do you remember an advert which used to be on the TV years ago. It was an advert for one of those healthy night-time milky drinks. It featured a man who had a clockwork key in his back, and as he went through the day the key began to wind his internal spring and as the day progressed it wound more and more tightly. It began, for example, with his alarm not going off and progressed from bad to worse. Every time something stressful happened the spring coiled even more tightly. By the end of the day he was shown tightly wound-up and collapsing in his arm chair. He then had a cup of this wonderful drink, which released his spring, and he became completely relaxed. I do not suppose many younger people have seen clockwork keys, it is all battery power and electronic gadgets these days. I have not seen the advert for years. But I think its a very graphic illustration of what is going on as we get more and more stressed throughout the day.

What I am going to teach you now is as relaxing as any health drink, milky or otherwise, and more beneficial because you do not have to wait until the end of the day to unwind. It is a simple breathing exercise to help you return to a normal breathing pattern, and once you have learned to do this, and can do it discreetly so that no one knows you are doing it, you can use it any time, any place. The result will be that you unwind, and feel calmer and more in control. It is taught to drama students to help them control stage nerves and I have used it myself before, and during, situations where I have wanted to keep calm. Here is how you do it.

Stress buster No. 2

Breathing exercises:

◆ Find a comfortable position in a quiet room, in a chair or on a bed.

◆ Relax as far as possible.

◆ Try to become aware of your own breathing and notice where the breath is in your chest cavity. The aim is to use your diaphragm, which is a flat muscle just under your lungs.

◆ Put your hands on your stomach and you should be able to feel the movement here.

◆ Breathe in for a slow count of three.

◆ Hold your breath for a slow count of three.

◆ Breath out for a slow count of three, flatten the stomach.

◆ Relax for a slow count of three, with shoulders forward and down.

◆ Repeat this rhythm two, or three times at first, gradually increasing the number of times, until you can breathe this way for as long as you need to, and as you do so imagine yourself slowly unwinding and letting go of everyday tensions.

◆ You can also increase the number of counts to more than three, as you get comfortable with the deeper breathing, or if you find three a strain try counting more quickly.

You will need to practice this at intervals throughout the day, every day, until you get the hang of it, then you can use it as an emergency stress buster when needed. Try to give yourself a reminder to do this just for one minute every few hours, each time you take a break for example.

If dizziness is a problem at first, do not worry, you brain is probably just not used to so much oxygen. Keep your eyes open and keep practising. It will pass. Another useful tip is to lie down when you first begin to practise and place a paper back book on your diaphragm so that you can check whether you are getting the breath in the right place.

But a word of warning. Do not wait until your first crisis situation occurs and then think, "Oh, I'd better use those breathing exercises". It will be too late then and you may be into a panic situation when the last thing you will want to do will be to recall something buried deep in your memory. You need to use it like a fire drill, practised often, and there when you need it.

Because you produce endorphins when you are relaxed you will probably start to enjoy the breathing. You will also find it very useful at the dentist, for example, not only to keep you calmer, but also to reduce the pain because endorphins are the body's own natural pain relievers. (Which is one of the reasons it is taught in ante-natal classes.)

When we are under stress our normal breathing pattern becomes disturbed. Have you ever noticed that when you are watching something exciting on the TV, or perhaps waiting for your team to score at a football match, you hold your breath? If you have reached stage two or three stress you may even find that breathing quickly and shallowly has become a habit, and learning to breathe more deeply requires quite a lot of practice at first. I have worked with people whose breathing has become so shallow as a result of stress that it has been difficult to see any chest movement at all. When you have mastered this technique you will find that you can be like the swan, gliding along, calm and unruffled, whilst still managing to get where you want to go. Your brain will remain focused and alert, directing your thoughts and your actions appropriately. Derek also found that he needed not only to check his breathing, but to give himself a quick body check at regular intervals and use a quick relaxation method to release his physical stress.

Many people are put off relaxation because they think they need to practise it lying down in a darkened room. This is a very good way to relax and I recommend it if you are willing to give it a go, but in this day and age of rush and bustle I find that most of the people who come to me for help want something which is immediate, and can be done in the midst of a busy day. Ours is the age of instant custard, fast foods, quick fixes and speedy responses. So here is a quick method of relaxation. You do not need to go into a darkened room, nor do you even need peace and quiet.

Stress buster No. 3

Relaxation (Laura Mitchell Method)[3]

◆ Choose the position you want to use, e.g. sitting or lying.

◆ If you are sitting, choose a high-backed chair, lean backward, or lean forward onto a table or desk.

◆ If lying down, lie on your side or your back. Make yourself suitably comfortable with pillows.

◆ Do not change the words, they are based on the fact that when you give yourself an exact order for movement, one set of muscles works and their opposite group relaxes automatically. That's what we want. You will find that the words fit any position you choose.

To change the pattern of stress to one of ease do three things each time:

1. Give an exact order to move the part.

2. Stop doing it.

3. Feel the new position.

Getting ready

"Place your hands and arms on the arms of the chair, or on your thighs if you are sitting down". If you are lying down place them flat on your tummy or thighs.

Shoulders and elbows

"Pull your shoulders down away from your ears, pull them all the way down."

Stop doing this, do not worry if the shoulders bounce up a bit, that may be because your upper muscles are a little shortened due to tension in the past.

Feel this position. Feel the length that comes into the back of your neck as a result.

"Push your arms away from you a little and make a wide angle at your elbows."

Stop. Allow your arms to fall back to your side.

Feel your heavy arms well supported, with elbows open and out.

Notice the open angle at your elbows and that your arms are away from your sides. Do not move, feel.

Hands

"Stretch your fingers, make them as long as you can. Make space between each finger so the hand becomes wide as well."

Stop. Let your hand flop back onto the support. Feel your fingers and thumb stretched out, separated and touching the support, with finger-nails on top. In particular feel your heavy thumbs.

Legs and feet

"Turn your legs outwards, so your knees and feet flop outwards."

Stop. Feel your heavy legs supported, push your toes away from you. Do it gently to prevent cramp.

Stop. Feel your heavy floppy feet. If you are sitting down the soles of your feet will be resting on the floor.

Body

"Push the small of your back into the chair or bed".

Stop pushing. Feel the support holding you up. Use it to take your weight.

Do it again. Feel your body resting on the support.

Head

"Push your head into the support."

If your head is not supported, try just pushing back as if there was an imaginary wall. The direction will be same as for the body support.

Stop pushing. Feel your head resting on the support. Leave it there. Your neck muscles will now release completely because your head is well supported.

Breathing

"Breathe at your own pace".

Breathe out fully and easily. Sigh if you wish. Breathe in gently, feeling your ribs lifting up and outwards. Breath out especially fully and easily, and your ribs will drop. Make no effort. Keep it very gentle. Feel it then forget it.

Face and head

Forehead

You are going to try to relax a cap-like muscle that encloses your skull just under your hair. When people are tense they often complain of the tension in this muscle as a tight band round the head. Because there is not any joint to work on, its rather difficult to get relaxation in it. Imagine you are stroking your fingertips from your eyebrows, across your forehead, up through your hairline and back. You may like to actually move your hand and do this the first few times. You may feel your hair move. Try again.

Jaw

Keep your lips closed, it is more comfortable.

"Drag your lower jaw downwards inside your closed mouth to separate your teeth".

Do it. When you feel the teeth separated, stop doing it and you will feel the cheeks are stretched, your jaw is free and your lips are loose. Do not drop the jaw drag it.

Stop doing it. Feel the result, especially your loose lips. Feel what your tongue is doing. If it is on the roof of your mouth pluck it off and make it lie in the middle of your mouth.

Stop. Feel it lying in the middle of your mouth.

Eyes

You may have already closed your eyes. If you haven't now is the moment to give the order "Close your eyes".

You close your eyes in one exact movement. You lower the eyelids. That's all you do. Stop doing it, and they stay there. If you do not feel like doing this at the moment do not worry. It is natural to feel a little nervous about doing it. Do not hurry. In time you will be able to do it. Feel the result. Feel the darkness that you have made. It is a very restful situation and the brain is at rest. You are in control. Teach yourself how restful, pleasant, and safe it can be. Feel it. Enjoy this relaxation you have created.

Direct your mind

While your body is fully relaxed it is important to direct your thoughts. Think of something enjoyable from past experience, preferably something with a sequence, perhaps a song or a poem. Or perhaps your favourite place, or food, something you have really enjoyed. It is important to think of the good side of life, and to reinforce the enjoyment and happiness.

Maintain this position for thirty seconds, use a timer if you like. Half a minute's rest can seem like a good long time when you are fully relaxed.

Now choose what you want to do next if you want to become a fully conscious human being again, open your eyes and slowly sit upright in a leisurely manner not quickly, and have a stretch. Or you may prefer to stay where you are having a prolonged rest. If you do, enjoy it, that's most important. It is the reward of your own work.

When you have become good at doing this, and enjoy it, allow yourself a longer and longer time, and use different positions.

Recovery

When you feel ready to come out of your relaxation, have a good stretch and, if you are lying down, roll onto your side and get up slowly.

Always stretch your limbs and body in all directions and yawn. Do not hurry. Sit up slowly and wait for a minute or two before standing up.

Like the breathing this relaxation can be done anytime, anywhere, and you can even do bits of it when it would be appropriate. You could just relax your shoulders for example, if you were sitting at a desk and just wanted to ease the tension in that part of your body. I find doing the shoulder and back movements when I am in a traffic queue very helpful, and the neck stretch is useful at the end of a hard day when I have been thinking a lot and holding the tension in my head.

If you are a busy person and find it hard to give yourself permission to relax for very long just take 30 seconds to do this, and notice how much better you feel as a result. Then, when you have given yourself permission to slow down for 30 seconds and have seen the benefits, you may find you can stretch the 30 seconds to one minute, then one minute to two minutes, and so on. You might even achieve 20 minutes after all! Use a kitchen timer, or set your watch alarm, if you are worried about all the other things you should be doing.

Your increased productivity after a period of relaxation will convince you of its value. Just give yourself permission to do it for 30 seconds.

Re-charging your batteries

I have a friend who has trained as a stress therapist. Her particular training has mainly been in the use of hypnosis to help people unwind and counteract the effects of excessive stress. Some people are afraid of hypnosis, as a result of watching stage hypnotists and being afraid of losing control and of being programmed. This fear may be unnecessarily exaggerated, but it is good to question the credentials of anyone practising these techniques, and get a recommendation.

Hypnosis is a form of trance, or state of altered consciousness, and most of us would admit to being in a trance at some time or other - when we are fully absorbed in a book, or a film, for example, particularly as we find ourselves re-living the plot with the hero or heroine. With one part of our mind we know it's a story, but with another part we believe we are there, and we are unconscious to the world around us. Hypnotism is a much deeper version of this and the subject (you) has much greater control than would appear.

Hypnotherapy helps a person by-pass the conscious mind to make hidden resources available in awareness. The conscious mind is not needed in the process - after all we probably got into this state of stress unconsciously! Hypnosis can be used to great effect, and can help you gain control of your mind.

What my friend does is use the power of words to induce and maintain an altered state and people contact her when they have run out of conscious resources. It is a way of reaching a situation in which the person is highly-motivated to learn from their unconscious. It is not a passive state, nor are her clients under her control. She and her clients cooperate together, and the way in which the client responds teaches her what she needs to do next.

However, it is possible to learn to use the power of language for ourselves, to produce a deep state of relaxation, a form of self-hypnosis. In this state you are fully in control and you can come back at any point.

You might like to try using the following "power nap" to recharge your batteries.

Power nap (from *The Joy of Stress* Peter Hanson)[3]

Just sit back and make yourself comfortable and allow your eyelids to close.

Take three deep breaths, in through the nose and out through the mouth.

As you listen to my voice you can pay attention to the growing feelings of relaxation and comfort in your body.

I am going to count for you from one to ten, and as I do...

you can imagine yourself travelling down an escalator, a lift, or even a staircase to your own private place of peace and tranquillity.

- ◆ one...
- ◆ just beginning ...
- ◆ letting relaxation spread through your scalp ...
- ◆ and your face ...
- ◆ and your neck ...
- ◆ going down deeper ...
- ◆ more relaxed ...
- ◆ down to tranquillity ...
- ◆ three ...
- ◆ arms and hands relaxing ...
- ◆ breathing easy ...
- ◆ four ...
- ◆ every breath guiding you to deeper relaxation ...
- ◆ closer to your special place ...
- ◆ free from stress and tension ...

◆ to your special, private place ...

◆ five ...

◆ further down ...

◆ stomach knots dissolving ...

◆ deeper relaxation ...

◆ calm ...

◆ comfortable ...

◆ six ...

◆ deeper still ...

◆ letting go of all cares and worries ...

◆ buttocks and thighs relaxing now ...

◆ relaxing deeply ...

◆ seven ...

◆ legs and feet relaxing now ...

◆ all the way down to the tips of your toes ...

◆ eight ...

◆ going deeper ...

◆ to your special private place ...

◆ totally calm ...

◆ more profoundly relaxed

◆ nine ...

◆ almost there ...

◆ drifting comfortably deeper ...

◆ ten ...

◆ stepping out into your place of calmness and freedom from stress ...

◆ enjoying the feelings ...

◆ letting them soak into every part of you ...

◆ just let yourself drift with these feelings for a short while, and enjoy them ...

◆ and when you are ready ...

◆ just come back up your escalator, or lift ...

◆ and bring these feelings with you ...

◆ ten ...

- nine ...

- eight ...

- seven ...

- coming back to your everyday state of alertness ...

- six ...

- five ...

- four ...

- three ...

- two ...

- refreshed and relaxed ...

- one.

The first few times that you try this you may like to get someone else to read the instructions for you, reading them slowly and evenly, allowing each pause to last for several seconds. Alternatively you could tape record it for yourself. Eventually you won't need the instructions, you will be able to use this power nap at any time when you need to re-energise yourself. The times I find it most useful are, for example, after a busy working day when I still need energy for the evening, or at lunch time when I need to re-charge for the afternoon.

You will find that there are lots of different methods of achieving relaxation. Having tried the ones I have suggested you might like to discover some different methods and it is possible to buy relaxation tapes from health food shops and large stationers. See if you could borrow them first from your local library or from a friend before you spend money on tapes you may not use.

Make sure you have learned methods of relaxation which you can use at any time and place when you need to unwind. It is not generally convenient to take a tape into work and relax on the office or on the factory floor! You should also realise that you are the person in charge of your relaxation, not the voice on the tape. Tapes should only supplement what you yourself can do.

Your aim should be to be able to recognise those times when you are tense and have a variety of methods that you feel confident with, which you are able to use, and which are appropriate to the situation. You will then be able to use your time in supermarket queues, for example, in traffic jams, in waiting rooms, and at other times when your body has to slow down, to do a quick body check and to release the tension. You will then be changing the stress response and its negative effects to the relaxation response, using those times productively for the health and healing of your body and mind. Then you really will be busy, doing nothing.

Relaxation skills are important, also important are skills to prevent build up of tension in the first place.   Amongst these skills are time management, and assertive communication skills. The next chapter will teach you how to use these to prevent some of your stress.

References

1. Greenberg, Jerrold S (1983) *Comprehensive Stress Management*, Wm. C Brown.

2. Mitchell Laura (1987) *Simple Relaxation - the Mitchell Method for Easing Tension*, John Murray.

3. Hanson, Peter (1986) *The Joy of Stress*, Pan Books, London.

chapter nine

Sharpening your axe

I believe that, whilst life can be a struggle, and is often painful, as I mentioned earlier, it is not what happens to you but what you do with what happens to you, that ultimately shapes your life. As Tony Robbins'says, "It is not not what we do once in a while that counts, but our consistent actions. And what is the father of all action? What ultimately determines who we become and where we go in life? The answer is our decisions. It is in these moments that our destiny is shaped. More than anything else, I believe our decisions not the condition of our lives determines our destiny."

This chapter gives an overview of time management and some tips for assertive communication. These are important skills which will help you become proactive rather than reactive in handling your stress, improving your decision-making skills and developing ways to change yourself.

Jonathan

The work's clock struck four. Jonathan checked his watch. "Four minutes fast, as usual", he noted. In just an hour's time the hooter would sound and there would be a mass exodus from the site. Cars, bikes, men on foot, and some women too. The building trade had several females in its ranks these days, plus the secretaries and telephonists they employed on site. "Secretary, there's a laugh," thought Jonathan, momentarily picturing the young trainee who typed his letters and took his phone messages.

"What wouldn't I give for one of those Girl Friday-types with an impeccable filing system, a degree in Information Technology, and an intimate knowledge of the building trade. It would make my life so much easier."

Tracy was willing enough, he acknowledged. "It is just that I haven't had time to train her properly, and this is her first job after all. I really need to make time to sit down with her and teach her about my job, go over the filing system with her, and help her to develop a routine. Not to mention teaching her how to take messages and make phone calls." Judging by her performance when he asked her to phone Sheridans' for prices on some plumbing equipment last week he wondered just how much experience she'd had on the telephone, and he noticed she always waited until he was out of the hut that they laughingly called his office before making any calls. Not that doing that was hard. His work as senior estimator took him all over the yard here, and out onto the various sites where they were working. He scarcely had a moment in the office, and when he did he found a huge pile of letters, phone messages, contracts, etc. all waiting for him. It was no wonder that he often forgot things and then ended up working overtime to try to avert a crisis because he had forgotten to include something in his estimate, or hadn't checked a price carefully enough.

He started to make his way back to the office now, ruefully contemplating the various jobs he really ought to try to get through before he knocked off himself. There was one thing he'd been able to improve on, recently. He'd just bought himself one of those pocket tape recorders to use whilst he was out of the office, so that whenever he came across a job he needed to do, was given a verbal message, or remembered someone he had to call, he would put a message on the recorder. He still felt a fool doing this and was aware of the surprise on the faces of the staff, but he knew he'd get used to that, and already he was aware of the lessening of tension. He no longer had to rely on his memory, or scrappy bits of paper when he got back to the office.

Tracy was muttering at the computer when he got back. She was attempting a mail merge and so far the computer had only churned out blank sheets. He tried to help but his own computer knowledge was fairly basic and he wasn't a lot of help so he gave up. Tracy would have to type all the envelopes, and insert the names by hand if necessary. Jonathan thought again that it might save time and effort in the long run if he asked permission for Tracy to go on a computer training course. He hated the thought of being without her, even for one day. But maybe it would be worth it.

Sitting himself at his desk he cleared a space in the midst of the assortment of papers and dirty coffee cups and set down his tape recorder. "I'll do the phone calls first", he thought, "whilst people are still in their offices, and then I'll do the estimates. If I do them out in long hand Tracy is sufficiently familiar with my handwriting by now to be able to put them on the computer tomorrow and with a bit of luck I can sign them and get them off in tomorrow's post. Yes, and one of the phone calls I'd better make is to Anne, and let her know I'll be late again to-night"

"Here is Edward Bear coming downstairs now, bump, bump, bump on the back of his head behind Christopher Robin. It is, so far as he is aware, the only way of coming down stairs. Although sometimes he feels there must be a better way, if only he could stop bumping his head long enough to think about it."

A.A. Milne.

Have you ever felt like that? That there must be a better way, but you are so busy bumping your head that everything else is knocked out of it, and you have not got the time anyway to devise a better way of coming downstairs. We usually promise ourselves that we will develop a better way, but often never get round to it.

Did you know that the reason employees are traditionally given a watch or a clock when they retire from work stems from the early days of timekeeping when often the only clock for an entire community was the giant clock above the mill or factory. In those days crafty bosses were not above tampering with the timepieces to make sure that they ran slowly during the day, and quicker after the factory closed. Employees were banned from bringing watches or clocks into the factory to prevent this being discovered. The presentation of the retirement clock symbolised the fact that time was now their own.[2]

Nowadays we each have our own timepieces and have more control of our own schedules but this has brought a different kind of problem. We have become driven people[3] who tend to define ourselves by things that can be counted - the amount of money we earn, the number of things we have made, the diplomas or degrees on the wall. But the things that matter the most are difficult to quantify - friendship, being a good parent, or having good health, for example.

Managing your time effectively means finding a good balance between these elements; it is just as much about knowing when to take a break as when to work hard. "Just as Pavlov's dogs learned to salivate inappropriately, we have learned to hurry inappropriately"[4]. I believe that the bells of modern life have become the telephone, the computer, the alarm clock, the watch, and the hundred and one self-inflicted expectations that we build into our daily routine. Some people do thrive when up against a deadline, but there is a point of diminishing returns, at which more speed means poorer quality.

It is easy to thrive on challenge, especially if you are the one in control. Others find the pressures harder to endure. Not long ago people were predicting an age of leisure, of a four-day week for all, and we were told that our greatest worry would be working out how to spend our unlimited free time. Things did not work out like that: mergers, downsizing and recessionary cost cutting mean that many employees find it hard to get a day off work or to leave for home before the cleaners arrive. No matter how much they yearn for a more balanced life, most are obliged to sacrifice personal and family life to gain promotion or even to safeguard their jobs. Over the past 20 years working hours have gone up and holidays have come down. Time spent commuting has risen by a full day each year, while holidays are down by three and a half days.

The workplace has been described as a marathon race in which a minority manage to spring across the finishing line, while the majority fall exhausted by the wayside. Just how many employees burn out behind the front runners depends to some extent on the corporate culture. If senior managers' view, worker productivity in terms of quality rather than merely the quantity of hours worked, pressures are usually more manageable.

Unfortunately intense global competition, and entrenched ideas about what it takes to be a team player, mean the majority of organisations continue to equate efficiency, loyalty and ambition with the length of the working day. With so many time pressures it is no wonder that insufficient time is a major factor in the causes of stress.

Learning to manage your time is not about working longer hours. It is not about getting more people to do more work without adequate salary increase, and cramming more into the working day. Time management should encompass the whole our lives, not just that bit of it that we get paid for. It is about enabling you to find more time for yourself and getting a balance in your life. It is about working smarter, not harder.

If you are suffering undue stress because you seem to have too much to do, cannot prioritise, and feel snowed under by time pressures, then it is important that you undertake some time management training, or read a time management book. Good time management will help you prevent and manage your stress. Life is not a rehearsal for some day in the future when everything will come together. Your life is now. What do you really want to do with it?

Time management should be a two-stage process. If you use this process properly it should mean that you spend time on the things that are going to get you what you want from both your work and private life. Have you ever spent the days just managing day-to-day problems and practical activities and gone home at the end of the day wondering just what you have accomplished?

I find Klaus Møller of Time Manager International's ideas very useful. He says time management should be like a tree, and you should start with the trunk[5].

The Trunk is made up of your major goals for the three main areas of your life career, relationships and personal. This is what your life is all about.

The Branches are your key areas - where you need to concentrate your efforts to reach your major goals, and get what you want in the main areas of your life.

The Twigs are the major tasks to be performed within each of your key areas. The actual results you want to achieve and the details.

The Pine Needles are all the practical activities, minor items, information and other practicalities necessary to complete your major tasks.

Møller's Pine Tree is detailed on the following page.

Diagram 13.

A System for Overview - Your Personal Pine Tree

based on an idea by Klaus Møller, Time Management International

1. **Trunk** - overall goals for private and work life.

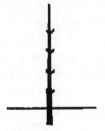

2. **Branches** - key areas (where you want to achieve results).

3. **Twigs** - major tasks, actual results you want to achieve.

4. **Needles** - practical activities, minor items, informations and details neccessary to complete major tasks.

Poor time management results from spending time managing the pine needles without being aware of the trunk and the key result areas. Before getting caught up in working out how you can do something in the most efficient way, you should ask yourself whether this is the right thing to be doing in the first place.

At this point you could look back to the priorities you listed in Chapter Three, and ask yourself, "If these are my priorities, what are the goals I need to set myself for each of these areas?" If you take time to plan your goals, your key areas and your major tasks on a regular basis, you will achieve more with your whole life, not just each working day. Use the planning sheet on the previous page to help you begin the process now.

The Pareto Principle applies here too. It suggests that as many as eight out of ten tasks which currently take up your working day are time wasters. So, in theory, we need to weed out the unproductive tasks. But be careful what you measure; time spent on seemingly unproductive tasks might be time when you are at your most creative. Some of your best ideas might come to you whilst you are doing one of the 80% so-called unproductive tasks such as standing at the photocopier or walking to lunch; or at home, taking a bath, walking the dog, lazing in the garden. How many times have you gone to an apparently unimportant meeting and met the person who introduced you to the person who gave you the tip that led to the most interesting job you have had so far? Give enough time by all means to the 20% of your work that you know to be productive, but leave some room for chaos and coincidence, synchronicity and serendipity.

Learning to prioritise is also one of the key skills in planning the working day. When asked how much of their daily work is urgent and important, people usually reply, "Everything I do is urgent and important!"

Prioritising needs you to challenge this statement, and you can do that with the aid of this diagram. Everything you do falls into one of the quadrants formed by the axes, as shown below.

Diagram 14. The Prioritising Quadrant

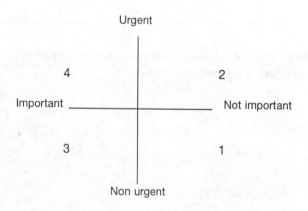

Quadrant 1 - not important and non-urgent

The first tip for successful time managers is to discover what tasks fall into this quadrant. Ask, "What would happen if I didn't do this?". If the answer is nothing, then why do it? You have identified a time waster. This quadrant could be labelled WASTE. Reading junk mail, and catalogues; completing surveys; dealing with people trying to sell you things you do not want, are all example of time wasters, and are things you do not need to do.

I am not talking about unimportant things that have to be done, irritants which you would rather not do, like opening the mail or doing photocopying. These are things which need to be done and go into Quadrant 2.

Quadrant 2 - urgent and not-important

These are tasks which have to be done, and have to be done urgently, but they are not important and therefore do not necessarily have to be done by you, or done to a very high standard. These tasks are QUICK AND SIMPLE. Devise a system for doing them quickly and getting them out of the way. Handle each piece of paper only once; action it, file it, pass it along or bin it! Use post-it notes for quick internal responses; use fax and send e-mails. Also consider batching these tasks, making several phone calls, sending all your faxes, doing all your photocopying at the same time, for example. Have an efficient filing system, and use it. But do not file those things which might come in useful one day. The average filing cabinet contains 60% of material which will never be referred to again. So only file if you are sure you will need it, and purge your files (both physical and computerised) regularly, making everything easier to find.

This is also an important area for delegation. But a word of warning, delegation is not the same as dumping. If you dump jobs which you do not want to do on a member of your team it is likely to be done badly, or not at all. With the task, delegate also the authority to do the task and as much of the whole task as possible so the person sees the end result or the purpose. This improves the interest and motivation factor. Most people enjoy being stretched and taking on a challenge when they can see the point of it. Being given responsibility is one of the satisfiers that increase people's enjoyment of their jobs.

Training too is important. Delegation often fails because the job is done badly or slowly without adequate checks built-in to the process. The manager then says, "It is quicker to do it myself!". Perhaps you have said this as a parent too. But employees, like our children, will never learn if we do not give them the responsibility, and we will end up always having to do that task, and supporting untrained, irresponsible staff. Training does take time, but if it is a job which has to be done often, then time spent training someone else to do it properly is time well spent. Remember the wood-cutter who spent all his time chopping down trees with a blunt axe, because he said he had not got the time to stop and sharpen his axe? Staff training is axe sharpening. Just as learning to manage your own time better is axe sharpening.

Delegation is not just about passing jobs onto junior staff, either. You may not have any staff at all, but you can still delegate. You can delegate to each other, and you can delegate upwards to your boss if you are clever.

If you are trying to balance more than one job, work and home for example, there are important areas for delegation here too. Involve family members in taking full responsibility for jobs at home; they are never too young to start. Consider also the goodwill of neighbours and family members, which might have been offered, for shopping and errands etc. Remember also the advice given in coping with work overload in Chapter Six. This leaves us with two more quadrants to consider.

Quadrant 3 - important and non-urgent

It is true that a large part of your day is likely to be spent dealing with urgent and important work, but if you did all your work as if it belonged in Quadrant 4 you would be operating in a crisis style of time management which is not a very efficient one. It leaves no time for real crises. Consider how much of your work you knew would become urgent. There was a report you had to write, but it was not needed until today so you delayed it. Now you're in the middle of it and the Chief Executive says he has to see you urgently, the computer has crashed, or the photocopier is out of order. You have not allowed for Murphy's Law, which says that "if anything can go wrong, it will go wrong"? (Bread always falls butter side down, for example.)

The key to successful prioritising is to think ahead to all of those important tasks which will one day become urgent and project plan them, for example.

◆ Give yourself a deadline for the completion of the job, allowing time for the operation of Murphy's Law.

◆ Break the job down into a series of tasks.

◆ Place these tasks in a logical order.

◆ Study the implications of each task.

◆ Estimate resource requirements (including time and staff implications).

◆ Set yourself a date for completion of each task.

These smaller jobs can now be done in Quadrant 3, which is Action Planning, and you will have time to do them properly, without mistakes. Mistakes take longer to correct than preventing them in the first place. So make sure that some of your day (dare I suggest 20%?) is spent in advance planning and making lists of everything you have to do.

Quadrant 4 - urgent and important

You should now have some time for the really urgent and important things - the crises which cannot be avoided. You can give them attention and deal with them well without a sense of panic. The inability to recognise our own rights and to stick up for them is also a major factor in time wasting. We misguidedly agree to help colleagues with jobs, take on more projects than we can cope with, allow ourselves to be coerced into sitting on committees and cannot even get rid of talkative colleagues who steal our time. I am talking here about the skills you need to be assertive and take care of yourself.

Assertiveness skills

Alix Kirsta[6] says that the most deep-rooted component of personality is our value system. It reflects how we rate ourselves in relation to others and see the world in general. It is learned at a very early age, and is often the most rigid and least flexible aspect of our personality. Our behaviour is a direct expression of these values and feelings and reflects our innermost attitude to ourselves. She believes that the origin of much personal stress lies within our perception or concept of self. If our self-esteem is low it can lead to a number of stress-inducing problems, such as inability to adapt, willingness to place excessively high demands on ourselves and lack of assertiveness. If we find it difficult to express ourselves, we are likely to harbour negative emotions such as anger, fear, aggression, and anxiety, rather than giving vent to them.

You can alter your perception of yourself. Lack of assertiveness usually has its roots way back in the past. You may still be responding to messages you were given by the important people in your life when you were very small. Such as: "Don't answer me back!", "Children should be seen and not heard", "Don't ask so many questions.", "Shut up!", "You have to do what I say." Some of these messages may have been implicit in the way we were brought up, rather than explicit.

As a child you responded to those messages, and played them unconsciously in your head. They were very useful to you, they kept you out of trouble and helped you win the approval of the grown-ups around you. It became a pattern. But there is no direct transition from childhood to adulthood; the process is gradual, and along the way you may not have realised that it is OK to discard childhood patterns and beliefs, and adopt more appropriate ones for adult life.

If you recognise this as something which is important for you then one of the first steps you can take is to listen more carefully to the inner messages you are playing to yourself, and begin to change them for more appropriate ones for adult life.

Begin by developing an understanding of what is meant by assertiveness. What does that word mean to you? Do you picture a dominant, vociferous, hard-nosed person, standing up for his rights, and getting what he wants by any means available? If so you are, in common with many other people, confusing assertiveness with aggression. Aggression is at the top end of the assertiveness non-assertiveness scale. At the other end is the shrinking violet who cannot say boo to a goose.

A useful definition of assertiveness is "the ability to stand up for one's rights, whilst being respectful of the rights of others". So assertiveness comes somewhere in the middle of the scale. It is a method of communication, and when we communicate with other people we can do so in one of three ways: we can raise, lower or level with them. If we raise the other person we do so in such a way that we are allowing them to assume a higher status than ourselves. When we praise other people, admire them, or encourage them we are raising them. (Also when we fawn, boot-lick and ingratiate ourselves). People do this because they feel that somehow the other person is more important than they are, which is useful when you are doing it deliberately to encourage someone else - children or junior colleagues for example. But in other settings you have to be careful that you do not come over as another Uriah Heep!

On the other hand when we bully, ignore, put down, and criticise we are lowering the other person. The hidden message is, "I'm better than you". People often do this to satisfy their own sense of being superior, but more often because they are not sure of their status and exaggeratedly try to ensure that the other person becomes aware of how important they or their opinions are.

When we level with the other person we are saying, "I have my rights and opinions, you have yours. I would like you to listen to what I have to say, and I am prepared to listen to what you have to say. Then we can talk about it, negotiate, compromise, or do whatever else is necessary to achieve a workable solution". This is assertiveness. It is direct, open, honest communication.

Oh, and by the way, getting your own way by manipulation, or devious means, whether by trickery or subterfuge, or flirting or seduction, is veiled aggression. People who do this usually lack the skills to be assertive and use these underhand means to get their own way, ignoring the rights of the other person. Assertiveness is direct, open, honest communication.

If lack of assertiveness is your problem, joining an assertiveness class, reading some books and practising, can all be good ways to develop your skills, and improve your communication as a whole and developing confidence to speak up when appropriate. Two important truths also go hand in hand with confidence. Let us take them one at a time.

First of all your brain does not process negatives. Often, when we want to change our behaviour we list the things we want to avoid. We say, "I must remember not to do that. I'll try not to blush, I'll try not to trip over my feet, and not to say anything about..." We go over in our minds the things we want to avoid, and then try to do something different, and wonder why it does not work. What you have done is given your subconscious a perfect blueprint of what you do not want, and because it has not processed the negative it thinks this is what you really want to do and assists you in reproducing exactly the same behaviour next time.

Try this. Say to yourself, "I will not think about my feet". What are you thinking about at this moment? Of course, your feet. Your brain did not process the word not. If you do not want to think about your feet you have to give your brain a positive message about what to think about instead. If you say "I will think about my hands", you direct your focus away from your feet.

When an important occasion is coming up, like a job interview, we tend to run over our previous experiences in our minds and remember all the stupid things we did, and play these negative messages? We go for the interview and we find it very, very difficult to behave differently no matter how hard we try. Why? The answer is simple we are rehearsing failure when we should be rehearsing success. So in order to behave differently you have to have positive images to rehearse.

The second truth is that the brain does not know the difference between fantasy and reality. It reacts as if you were actually in the job interview whilst you are thinking of it, so you become aware of sweaty palms, butterflies in the stomach, etc. etc.

To illustrate my point just take a moment to think of a slice of lemon, a nice juicy lemon, imagine yourself holding it, slicing into it, and then taking one of the slices and putting it to your lips, tasting it, savouring the sharp tang of the lemon..... What is happening? Are you salivating yet? I'll bet you are, and yet there is no lemon in sight. The only one is in your mind, from which your brain is taking its stimulus.

When you rehearse negative behaviour it becomes a self-fulfilling prophecy which your brain is only too happy to reproduce. If you want to behave differently or have a different emotion create pictures of yourself behaving in a different way, even modelling yourself on someone you know who can do this well, and practising a new way.

Giving yourself a break, having the courage to examine long-held beliefs, to challenge and possibly change your attitudes toward yourself, your work, and your relationships, may in turn alter your whole relationship to stress.

Recognising that you have the right to make mistakes, to refuse excessive demands, to say no, to express your needs and feelings openly, to make time for yourself, and to cater for your wants as well as those of others all these are central to cultivating a healthy, balanced sense of self-altruism, probably the most basic survival skill of all. Learning to give yourself a break, in every sense of the word, takes practice, especially when you are the one who is driving yourself the hardest. But the rewards in terms of gaining self-possession, and restoring the feeling that you have control over your life, can prove incalculable.

In the next chapter we will look at other ways of giving yourself a break.

References

1. Robbins, Anthony (1992) *Awaken the Giant Within*, Simon and Schuster, London.

2. Lewis, Dr David (1995) *10 Minute Time and Stress Management*, Piatkus, London.

3. Wolff, Jurgen (1996) *"Creative Time Management"* in *Brainstorm*, published by Brainstorm, 85 Ridgmount Gardens, London CW1E 7AY.

4. Dossey, Larry (1982) *Space, Time and Medicine*, Routledge.

5. Møller, Klaus *The Time Manager*, BBC Training Video.

6. Kirsta Alix (1986) *The Book of Stress Survival*, Union Paperbacks, London.

chapter ten

All work and no play

I remember writing out in my best handwriting for a teacher at school, "All work and no play, makes Jack a dull boy". I have not heard anyone quote it for years. Do they still use these old saws in school I wonder? It is certainly as true today as it was when it was first written. I would guess it might be a Victorian quotation, one coined to counteract the work ethic which might have been in danger of turning men into machines. Nowadays it is not so much the danger of becoming a dull boy which concerns us, but more the danger of suffering from stress-related illness if we do not play a little more, and switch off from work at regular intervals. Leisure activities, regular breaks and recovery strategies are all extremely important in reducing stress levels.

Martin

Martin closed his study door. The sound of the television and children's voices receded. He switched on his computer and began to sort his papers whilst it booted up. He did not mind having to take work home in the evening. It gave him something to do as an alternative to television, which in the early part of the evening was hogged by the children anyway. It also provided an excuse for retreating into his den away from the children and Jane. This was the bit he did feel guilty about when he allowed himself to think about it. The Jane that he had married ten years previously had long since been replaced by a stern-faced, querulous woman whom he did not recognise sometimes. Where was that fresh, eager and attractive girl he had once been passionately in love with? Nowadays there was always something wrong - one of the children had a problem at school, she wanted him to put up a shelf, or do some decorating, or go shopping with her. Often she was nagging him to come home from work earlier so that she could go out, and if he did not manage it there would be a long face and sullen silences for the rest of the evening, sometimes even longer. There was one memorable occasion when she missed something or other and she did not speak to him for three days! They only started to speak then because they were due to go on holiday.

Holidays, now there was another thing. Jane had already started to talk about where they might go this year. How was he going to break it to her that he wouldn't have time for more than a week at most, and even that was doubtful. There were so many things happening at work right now. He just couldn't take the time off. He wondered if Jane would be willing to take the children away on her own? He anticipated more rows and long faces when he suggested it.

Didn't she realise how hard he was working for them all? She wouldn't have her dress allowance, or all the designer gear demanded by two fashion-conscious schoolgirls if he did not work so hard.

He had obtained two promotions in the last five years and was now marketing manager for the company, who sold computers and associated hardware. He would be in line for another promotion this year if all went well. The least Jane could do would be to keep the house efficiently, and look after the girls. Why did she need to be going to evening classes? What use would it be to her to be able to speak Spanish? She'd even been talking about getting a part-time job recently. Wasn't one bread-winner in the family enough? She knew he did not want her to go out to work.

He and Jane had two young children, both girls, and both full of energy and life. Every weekend they were off to gymnastics, horse-riding or some other event. He was once a keen sportsman himself; cricket had been his passion and once he had inspirations to play for the local team. But not any more; he'd had to cry off too often to be even considered.

Martin was a good provider for his family. He was proud of the home they had managed to buy, and there was a new car with the job. The trouble was there did not seem to be the time to enjoy the lifestyle they could now afford. His last promotion gave him added responsibilities as well as increased income and he always took work home to enable him to keep up. He was worried and anxious most of the time and felt that in order to demonstrate his worthiness for the promotion he had to work harder than any of his staff.

His manager was a hard task master too. He was probably a workaholic. Martin had never seen him take a lunch break. He was always in the building before any of the other staff, and no one knew what time he went home. He was a hard act to follow and his very example put pressure on the rest of the staff.. There were times when Martin longed for a genuine illness so that he could take some time off without feeling guilty. Perhaps a dose of 'flu? But, would it be worth it? The work would only pile up whilst he was away, and goodness only knows what the staff would get up to whilst he was off. They needed him there to keep them in order.

The workforce work longer hours in Britain than in any other European country. The only people with plenty of leisure time seem to be the unemployed, and they have too much of it, which in itself can cause stress. Everything in life has the potential to be stressful and even the most enjoyable job can cause problems if we do not set ourselves limits and sensible time scales.

Stress is also caused by unavoidable life crises which face us all. In addition there are potential sources of stress dictated by your own particular lifestyle. These can be far less obvious than the major life crises but can have a cumulative, pervasive effect. This is more likely to occur if you find yourself caught against your will in a certain way of life or if you cannot shape and amend your lifestyle to suit your needs.

It is easy to ignore minor symptoms, to deny their significance, or go for fast relief, using headache tablets, indigestion remedies, alcohol, cigarettes, etc; especially if you view your stress symptoms as a necessary price to achieve your career goals or maintain your lifestyle. Whilst fast relief of symptoms may have value in the short term, for longer-term health it is necessary to take more preventive action.

What really makes a difference is when you listen to the messages your body is sending you. After a little practice you can get very good at this. Then when you spend some time out of the physical stress response, in relaxation of one form or another, your body and mind have an opportunity to be renewed. You can regain your energy and develop a new focus.

Just as you are unique in your experience of stress and your response to pressure, stress management techniques are very personal too - it is important to discover what works for you. Your choice will depend on the nature of the stressor, your own likes and dislikes, what fits into your lifestyle etc.

I have heard Dr Cary Cooper talking about the need for a third life[1] and I think that is a good way of describing our play or leisure life. This third life gives us a space where we can involve ourselves in things which help us switch off the stress response, giving us a sense of satisfaction and helping to build up our inner resources. We may not realise that when we involve ourselves in a game of badminton, or join other volunteers restoring a steam railway, we are switching off the stress response, but that is what is happening. Everyone needs this, particularly if some aspect of life is stressful.

You may already have a third life or the beginnings of it, and not realise it. What are your hobbies and interests, what do you like to do to help you unwind at the weekends or in the evenings? Think about these and write them down here:

My hobbies and interests:

....

....

....

....

Next have a look at the activities that you have listed. Does this look like a third life or good list of things that will help you build this up? Do you take any exercise? Anything from walking the dog to training for the Olympics is exercise and can make a valuable contribution to stress management. There are great physical benefits: a decrease in anxiety and an enhanced sense of well-being which can be developed through exercise. You can make a significant difference by building short periods of activity into your existing lifestyle – walking up stairs rather than taking the lift; or parking the car a little further from work. You can also make sure you get your exercise when the dog gets his. (You will also find some more information on exercise in Chapter Eleven).

What do you do that makes you feel really relaxed? Do you read, listen to music, play a musical instrument, go fishing, for example. It does not matter what it is as long as it absorbs you and switches off the stress response, and when you do your body check during that activity you are aware of feeling relaxed. Even small things like taking a warm bath can promote relaxation, as also can some of the activities listed later under "small delights".

Man (or woman) is a social animal, and most of us enjoy socialising in the company of like-minded others. Has your list included some activities which take you into the company of friends or people who enjoy the same things as you do, with whom you can unwind? Having friends round and visiting them can be very relaxing and is often neglected when we are under pressure. Your hobbies or your particular form of exercise might involve meeting others, and you can achieve two objectives at once. Try also to ensure that your social circle includes people who are from a different occupation to yourself so that you can avoid talking shop when you socialise. This can be a particular problem if your partner also does a similar job. Above all do not allow your life to become so busy that there is no time to keep friendships in good repair.

Which of these things could you do over the next month, or two months? Take a few moments to jot down those which appeal to you and which you believe you could find room for, then include the date and time when you will start. Commit yourself to implement one or two this week.

It is important also to have some support in your life. Support from other people and support from yourself. This means that you should have one or more persons whom you can trust and who have a positive regard for you. These will be the people who are willing to listen to your concerns, to give emotional and sometimes practical assistance in times of need. In relationships we can both give and receive support. Providing support is one of the most important things we can offer our friends, family and colleagues, and returning their support of you can also be very rewarding and build up your self-esteem.

Knowing the people, activities and things that are important to you gives you an inner benchmark with which to assess the options you encounter and to make the choices that are right for you, maintaining your sense of proportion. This will help you keep closely in touch with your own values and increase the satisfaction that you get from your life.

We all have a spiritual side which should not be neglected either. Some will find this through prayer or meditation. Others will find it contemplating nature - a sunset, or a view; listening to uplifting music; reading poetry or beautiful prose; walking on a beach or in the countryside; listening to birds; and in many other ways. Look out for the things which nourish and sustain you and make life worthwhile. These are the things that make you smile, or sigh with relief, or gasp with amazement. Get into the habit of looking for these. You may find some inspiration for new ones in the following list.

Small Delights[2]

Keep a diary - count your blessings

Play a musical instrument

Join a relaxation/yoga class

Use the stairs instead of the lift

Listen to uplifting music

Dance around the kitchen

Watch the sunset

Plant a window box

Run on the beach

Look for something good in everyone you meet

Get up early and enjoy the quiet

Go for a walk

Make a list of all your good qualities

Stop and smell the roses

Set one short-term goal for self-improvement

Accept a compliment without apologising

Have a relaxing massage

Reward yourself for reaching a goal

Take ten deep breaths

Have a lie-in

Join an art or pottery class

Spend a weekend in the country

Recycle your newspapers and bottles

Stop smoking, starting right now

Decide today to begin taking care of yourself

Clean out a cupboard

Give your old clothes to a charity shop

Visit someone in hospital

Do something for someone less fortunate, for example become a blood donor

Weed the garden

Look at the clouds

Walk in the snow, or barefoot in the sand or on the grass

Try herb tea

Listen to the rain

Go to the beach

Listen to children

Laugh at yourself

Watch a funny video

Watch the sunrise

Buy some new clothes

Hug a child

Eat out

Dine by candlelight

Sit by the fire

Have a good cry

Write a poem

Sing in the bath

Read a novel

Go to the zoo

Go for a bike ride

Day dream

Take a day off

Live a little

As well as our leisure activities we should not neglect the importance of regular, sensible breaks. Taking a break from the situation can help you get into your mental helicopter and rise above the situation and view it differently. It also helps to switch off the stress response.

Plan a mini-holiday; spend some time planning it and savouring what you will do. Read about the places you will be visiting. Bring back a lovely memento, some postcards, take photographs, anything which will serve as a reminder of your time out and sustain you in the weeks up to your next break We should view our leisure as down time, a time when we are building up our body's mental and physical resources to cope better with the stresses of our life.

Make sure you take your holiday allowance too, it is something to which you are legally entitled. Many people I have spoken to, for example university lecturers (no, they do not all have three months off in the summer!) find that their holiday allowance gets eaten into by extra courses, marking, assessment boards and so on. They reach the end of the academic year without having taken a holiday. It is then difficult to get the holiday they are entitled to because lectures are beginning again. This is a dangerous (to your health) situation to allow yourself to get into no matter what your job is. You may need to book your holiday well in advance and be strong-minded about taking it regardless of what happens in your job.

Many people do not take holidays, or even days off, because they believe they are indispensable, and that no one else could stand in for them, or the work would suffer. When I meet people who have that attitude I offer to let them try the indispensability test. This test has never been known to fail. It involves a bucket of water. People who are indispensable can put their hand in the bucket of water and when they remove their hand there will be a space remaining where their hand should be! I have not met anyone yet who passed this test. Apply it for a moment in your life. If you were to meet with an accident or develop a fatal illness, your employers may be very sad to lose you, but their main concern is the job you do. Someone else will quickly be found to cover for you and the job will be advertised without delay. The people who would really suffer are your family, who are more dependent on you. So you need to be concerned about staying healthy, taking care of your stress, and making sure you are always there for your family and your employers.

Talking of breaks, it is not just holidays which are important. Advice given to today's stressed executives is to take regular short breaks rather than waiting for the annual six weeks in the sun. Many people doing jobs which are highly stressed have recognised this need and have weekend retreats such as caravans, holiday cottages, boats, etc. to which they can escape regularly. If you own a cottage or a boat you feel the need to use it as often as you can to justify the expense so you are almost forcibly removed from the work situation to one that is more restful and diverts your thoughts elsewhere. There are different schools of thought about whether you should take work with you to your holiday cottage. Ideally you should not. Your retreat should be just that, a place away from the phone and the demands of work. But if you have to take a report for preparation, or a pile of marking, for example, at least you are doing it in a restful situation, away from the phone and day-to-day pressure. I have developed a habit of taking only routine stuff such as marking, but always try to avoid taking anything which requires me to shut myself away from other people whilst I do it.

Those who take regular mini-breaks notice the difference it makes. Marian is a Project Development Officer with a large public company. She took this advice. She and her husband began taking a weekend away every six weeks. They did not have a cottage or a caravan, so sometimes they found a cheap weekend break somewhere; sometimes they just visited friends or relatives, or got out for a day in the countryside. She said, "At first I used to feel guilty about the work I was leaving behind. I always took work home at the weekend that I hadn't been able to finish during the week. But then I discovered that after a break I could get down to the task re-energised and with a clearer head and get it finished in half the time it would normally take me."

You do not have to be rich either. You do not have to own a boat or a caravan. You can plan weekends with friends. In these days of increased mobility a lot of us have friends who live in other parts of the country, even abroad. Invite them to spend a weekend with you if you have not been invited to stay with them. You will then enjoy a weekend taking them to places in your own locality that you'd been promising to visit for ages and never got round to. You will almost certainly be invited to visit them in return.

If you do not have friends to visit, you could plan a weekend at home as if you had friends with you. Visit museums and parks, explore local footpaths, go to a show, do one of those countless things you have always been promising yourself to do. Spend some time with members of your family and keeping in touch with old friends. Discover how many things there are to do and places to visit in your locality which do not cost anything.

If your life is stressful you will need to make this a definite plan of campaign otherwise work may take over. Even breaks of a few hours can be very effective in the middle of a period of pressure, allowing yourself a half day off, or a longer lunch break. Do not neglect your regular breaks during the working day. Take the lunch break you are entitled to, and if you cannot get away from the telephone at lunch-time, sit in your car to eat a sandwich, and listen to the radio.

Your source of stress may be one which is ongoing such as caring for a handicapped child, or parent, like the example below. This is when leaving the situation for just short periods of time is absolutely vital.

Pamela

Pamela cares for her invalid mother who makes enormous demands on her time and her energy, her patience and her love. At this stage Pamela is not willing to consider a nursing home as an option, so she handles her stress by getting away for short periods as often as she can. Her local social services provide a night sitter once a week, and Pamela pays the same person to come for an extra night, so that she can get out for two evenings. She goes to a Yoga class where she can restore her energy and relax, and she is learning to play Bridge at evening classes. On both occasions she meets other people who share her interests and help her to keep a perspective on her situation. Once every six weeks her sister, who lives 65 miles away, comes to stay for the weekend and Pamela goes walking with the local rambling group or has a weekend away with friends. Pamela has learned to do this and not feel guilty, because by getting away at regular intervals she returns restored and is able to continue with the heavy burden of caring in a more cheerful and positive way. Sometimes one of her mother's friends will drop in for a chat and when they do Pamela pops to the shops or the library for an hour. She makes every opportunity to care for herself as a person, so that she can continue to have the resources she needs to care for her mother.

You may feel that you want to get away from your stress completely by resigning your job or leaving a relationship. But before you consider this option, look very carefully at the source of the stress and the way you are handling it, and ask yourself whether you might be able to handle it differently if you developed your skill. If you try everything within your power, using the advice you have been given in this book and any other resources you may have, only then should you consider walking away from the situation. After all, as President Truman said, "If you cannot stand the heat, get out of the kitchen". But just walking away from a situation that causes stress is not always the right option. Certainly it removes the stress at a stroke, but what then? It does not do anything to improve your ability to handle stress, and it may leave you with the feeling that you have failed. You may feel that you should have tackled that bullying boss, or been able to cope better with the long hours of work. You may go on to another job and find the same problems develop there. If you have not learned some coping skills you are likely to end up just as stressed.

But when you have tried everything else and leaving the situation seems to be the only option – go for it. There is life beyond what you are doing as many people will testify. You never know whether you might be able to get another job until you have tried. I have met people who have changed careers, taken courses of study, retired early, and just opted out. Often they have done this quite late in life and some of them, sadly, as a result of major stress-related illness. Someone who successfully got away from a stressful job is Celia, whom I first met when she was giving a talk to a women's group on colour and image. She told me that she had once been a teacher. "But I couldn't take the long hours, the budget cuts, the continual changes, the staff shortages. It was affecting my health. I had a friend who was an image consultant and she told me how she got started. I looked into it and discovered that I could take up a franchise with one of the major organisations and that training was available. I had always had a good eye for colour and decided to give it a try. Three years later I am still enjoying it and getting enormous satisfaction from it. I love the flexible hours and being my own boss. It took a lot of courage to take that first step, and I was very scared but I did it anyway."

A third life and regular breaks are all important strategies which will help you to recharge your physical and emotional batteries. I think it was Snoopy who said, "There is no problem so big it cannot be got away from!" So resolve to plan your leisure activities and your breaks starting now.

References

1. Cooper, Cary, *Stress* (Master Class) Video, Melrose Films, London.

2. Based on training material used by Howard Clinebell at a conference for the Clinical Theology Association in 1986.

chapter eleven

Food and mood

"First and foremost stay healthy. Watch your diet. Exercise."[1]

Sal F Marino, Chairman Emeritus of Penton Publishing Inc.

The connection between what we eat and our disposition is rarely recognised yet can have a profound effect. One of the most obvious changes you can make to improve your ability to withstand stress is to improve your diet.

Like all animals, humans were designed to assume that food is scarce, not that there would be unlimited supplies of highly calorific food at all times. Advanced capitalism exploits our instinctive animal tendency to overeat fats and sugars, when what most of us need is plenty of roughage and a lot less calories. Having overeaten, we come to hate our shape and to resent our ponderous bodies, and so we can be sold diet products. Or we may starve ourselves. All of these factors result in poor dietary habits affecting not only our weight, but our mood and the degree of stress we can withstand.

Kathy

Kathy was an infants' school teacher. She was also a wife and mother, and like so many school teachers she put 100% into everything she did. She was the first up, she fed the family, planned the evening meal, gathered together the PE kit, the dinner money, the packed lunches, and the many other small items that children need for the day. She made sure her husband had his clean shirt, helped him find his car keys; and assembled her own class work which she had been working on the night before. She next drove half a mile to drop the children off at their own school and then six miles in the opposite direction to her own school. In all of this, getting some breakfast for herself was a minor consideration, and in any case she was already too wound up to digest anything. So she had got out of the habit of eating first thing and didn't worry about it because she wanted to keep her weight down anyway.

She spent a hectic day teaching, and dealing with all the necessary paperwork as well as the hundreds of problems with which her young pupils presented her. Lunchtime was usually spent tidying the classroom, putting work out for the afternoon, giving attention to classroom displays, dealing with children's problems, meeting parents, or quite often attending a necessary staff meeting.

Sometimes during all of this she managed to eat an apple or a banana, but little else.

After school she would collect her children from a neighbour who had met them from school, and take them home to begin preparing a meal for them all. Her children were always hungry after their busy day and could never wait for their meal. The constant cry was, "What's to eat, Mum?". Somehow no matter what they ate on arrival home, they still had appetite for the meal which Kathy prepared in time for Chris when he got in. By this time, in spite of the cup of tea and biscuit that Kathy had had when she got in, she was usually feeling light-headed and tired. She was always snappy and irritable too and her children often got the rough edge of her tongue By the time the family meal was over and the washing up done, all Kathy wanted to do was slump in front of TV and no matter how hard she tried she usually found that she fell asleep. It became Chris's job to put the children to bed. It was a monumental effort for Kathy to spend any time in the evening on lesson preparation, and more often than not most of it was left until the weekend when she could find more energy.

What Kathy was doing was the equivalent of trying to run a car without putting any petrol in the tank. She was trying to drive her body without any fuel for the energy she needed. herself. She started the day with nothing in her energy bank and continued to make withdrawals throughout the day. It's no wonder she was fit for nothing at the end of the day.

What did Kathy need to do to change this around and regain her energy? We need to look at the body as a system which produces the energy needed to keep going throughout the day. Our foods are the fuel which keeps it going. To use another analogy, we put fuel on a fire to produce heat (and heat is a form of energy). When we want quick heat from the fire we put on something that will burn quickly, such as wood, or even paper, depending on how quickly we want to revive it. If we want the fire to go on burning for a longer period of time without attention, we use coal, coke, anthracite, or other long-burning fuel.

When I was a small child, growing up in the 1940s, we depended on the fireplace for our heating and our cooking, so keeping the fire burning was very important. My mother taught me how to use "nutty slack" on the fire before going to bed, so that the fire would still be burning in the morning. (If you have never heard of "nutty slack", it is small particles of coal, and coal dust, which take a long time to burn.)

In a job which demands high levels of activity, whether mental or physical, you need to use these same principles to take account of the energy needs of your body. Your body needs its own equivalent of nutty slack. Athletes know about the value of adequate nutrition and high energy foods. Few people realise that, even if we do not expend vast amounts of physical energy, our brain still uses energy and needs nutrition. Just as you need to keep supplying a fire with fuel, so you need to supply your body with energy foods which will produce the energy you need on a daily basis. You need to understand how and when to give your body what it needs. Not only that, you need to remember to maintain adequate nutrition by topping up your energy bank at regular intervals, If you do not, you end up running on your nerves, rather than your food resources.

When I taught Kathy these important truths she began by ensuring that she had a nutritious snack available at lunch time, she packed a sandwich made with wholemeal bread to accompany her apple, and had fruit and nut bars, muesli bars, etc. available for other quick snacks rather than sweet stuffs. She also began to re-educate her body to eat breakfast. She said, "Chris laughed at me at first, because I bought a packet of wholewheat breakfast cereal and on the first day I was only able to force down just one tablespoonful. But, I gradually increased this until I was able to eat a whole bowlful. He does not laugh anymore, because I've stopped falling asleep in front of the TV every night and I'm taking my turn at putting the kids to bed!" Kathy also found that she was less tired during the day and by teatime on Friday she still had some energy left. As long as she remembers to eat at lunchtime too, she no longer gets the light-headedness and pounding headaches which were once inevitable ends to every working day. She gets through most of her marking and preparation during the week, and her children get some of her energy at the weekend.

Professor Andrew Smith at Bristol University has said that eating breakfast is pleasurable, legal, improves your memory, boosts your mood and may even make you more attractive to the opposite sex. He maintains that regular breakfasting improves your happiness, and that breakfast cereal eaters are slimmer than abstainers.

But not all cereals are healthy and provide nutty slack. A major supermarket chain has arranged them in order of their healthiness, starting with the saintly porridge oats, Shredded Wheat, and Ready Brek, moving through the tolerably good (muesli, Weetabix, and Corn Flakes), finishing with products that are hard to call healthy: Sugar Puffs, Coco Pops, Frosties and many other children's cereals. Do not be misled by claims of healthy and sporty products; read the labels and compare the nutritional labels, and remember cereals are only part of your diet. Claims to lower cholesterol and low fat are only valid when taken into consideration alongside other foods that you eat, and also bear in mind the high sugar content of many of these products.

One of the problems with our modern diet is that food is too easy. We eat a lot of junk foods without thinking about the need for a balanced diet. Some of the most destructive substances actually form part of our diet. Chemicals in many of our foods, drinks and drugs, contribute to stress. Salt increases nervous tension, fluid retention and blood pressure, and it is thought that hyperactivity in some children is linked to food additives. A dietitian friend of mine maintains that if sugar were introduced as a new food today, it would be banned because it is so unhealthy. A healthy diet should include protein, fats, carbohydrates, fibre, vitamins and minerals, and water.

Protein foods are meat, eggs, cheese, milk, fish, etc. These should make up about

15-20% of your total calories. There is no need to carefully weigh everything. Just take a look at your plate and check the proportion of protein to everything else. It is found in most foods, not just meats. Excess protein in the diet will be converted to fat, and this is true of all foods. It can also cause decreased calcium resulting in bone thinning. So it is important to keep to a sensible amount. The typical Western diet contains far more protein than our bodies really need.

Fats should form 30 to 35% of total calories. Fats are, of course, butter, cheese, oils, fatty fish, animal fats. A balanced diet should contain both animal and vegetable fats. Trying to reduce your fat intake is sensible, trying to cut it to nothing is a mistake. We need fats because they are essential components of our immune system and our vulnerability to illness is greater when the immune system is lowered.

You may be concerned about high cholesterol levels from your fat intake. Studies have shown that a more important factor in high cholesterol levels is stress, rather than diet. If you do not handle your stress well, and stress-proof yourself, you will probably show high cholesterol levels. In the West, working long hours, meeting deadlines and targets, struggling to manage the home and a job, etc. are big stress factors which reduce our feelings of control in our own lives. Large amounts of cholesterol are deposited in our arteries as a result.

However, fibrous foods, such as vegetables and cereals, act as a sponge to fat. If you eat enough (50 grams per day) the fibre will absorb the fat and assist in the excretory process. Cholesterol levels will then decline.

Fat is also important for energy storage, and for storage of the fat-soluble vitamins (A,D,E and K) as well as providing us with an insulation layer in winter. But beware, when the diet is high in fat it is far too easy to consume too many calories, as fat has nine calories to the gram, whereas proteins and carbohydrates are only four calories per gram. Beware also the hidden fats in gravy, meat, chicken skin, as well as the fat in the cooking process itself, particularly fried foods.

Diagram No. 15

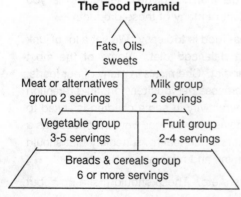

The Food Pyramid

Fats, Oils, sweets

Meat or alternatives group 2 servings | Milk group 2 servings

Vegetable group 3-5 servings | Fruit group 2-4 servings

Breads & cereals group 6 or more servings

The best diet for stress is one that:

- Natural - as few additives as possible
- Containing the right number of calories to maintain your ideal body weight
- Eaten at a reasonable pace, and at regular times
- Balanced - see The Food Pyramid

Making protein the smallest portion at a meal can double your energy output and endurance

In terms of energy the most important foods are the carbohydrates, and for many people it is the realisation of how sugar behaves in our bodies, particularly when we are stressed, that helps them understand how they are contributing to their own stress levels, and how by simply changing what and how often they eat they begin to feel more energised and healthy.

When the stress response is triggered, the liver releases sugar to provide us with extra energy. So people under stress have higher than usual blood sugar levels (hyperglycaemia). Insulin is then produced to deal with this and the sugar levels fall. We notice this drop and rush for a biscuit or a chocolate bar to raise our sugar levels again, being unable to wait for our blood sugar to rise again naturally when we have eaten. This results in a blood sugar which peaks and troughs and can become unstable as a result. Diabetes can be triggered or even caused by stress in this way. What we need to do is to ensure that we eat a diet rich in complex carbohydrates, and low in simple carbohydrates. The complex carbohydrates are converted into sugar by the digestive system and the blood sugar rises naturally, and is maintained naturally so long as we continue to eat regularly, and to eat the right foods. Hypoglycaemia is another cause of fatigue and irritability.

Diagram No. 16

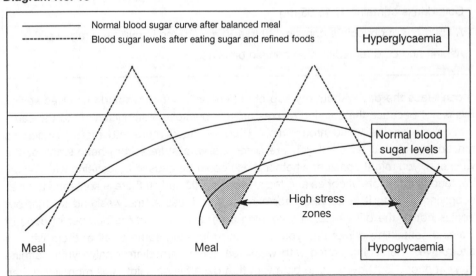

	Normal blood sugar curve after balanced meal
	Blood sugar levels after eating sugar and refined foods

Hyperglycaemia

Normal blood sugar levels

High stress zones

Meal

Meal

Hypoglycaemia

Factfile No. 6

Carbohydrates

Complex carbohydrates = whole wheat foods, vegetables, fruit, pasta, pulses (lentils etc.) whole grain cereals.

Simple carbohydrates = refined sugar, white flour.

Caffeine

Another baddie as far as what we eat is concerned is caffeine. Caffeine is found in coffee, tea, cola drinks and chocolate, for example. Caffeine is a stimulant (of the heart and nervous system). An article in the *British Medical Journal* referred to caffeine as "the world's most popular drug". Many people are unaware of the full effect that caffeine has on their physical and psychological health. When you are under stress the last thing you need is something that is affecting you in a negative way.

Coffee's mental lift has been known about since the ninth century when an Arab herdsman named Kaldi noticed that after his goats had eaten certain berries they got on their hind legs and danced! In 1511 it was put on trial in Mecca, banned and burned. Today it is merely lightly roasted, then freeze dried.[1]

Factfile No. 7

Caffeine

Coffee contains about 90mg caffeine (instant), 200 mg (filter)

Tea contains about 40 to 100 mg depending on strength

Cola drinks contains 40 to 65 mg

A 150g bar of chocolate contains 30 to 100 mg (30 mg in milk, 100 mg in plain)

Aspirin and cold remedies also contain caffeine.

"I can't face the day without my cup of coffee/tea". When we find ourselves saying this is not because the caffeine relaxes us, it is because it stimulates us to the same crazy pace as the world around us. Then we need more and more to keep us functioning at that level. If you are someone who suffers from headaches at the weekend, you might consider whether these could be caused by caffeine withdrawal. We tend to drink lots of coffee and tea at work, particularly if there is someone to keep supplying us with it (a secretary for example) and less at the weekend so that our bodies notice the difference. Try keeping a careful count of the number of cups of caffeine-containing drinks that you have, and replacing some or all of them with an alternative. Replacing coffee with weak tea could immediately halve your caffeine consumption. But you need to be aware that decaff is no saint. It is more likely than coffee to cause stomach irritation, as well as raise cholesterol levels.

If you are a real coffee addict you might try first of all switching to strong tea, using tea bags and a metal container which will help reduce the amount of caffeine. You could then gradually make your tea weaker and weaker. You could also try replacing some of the tea drinks with healthier alternatives such as herbal tea, pure fruit juice, or mineral water.

Sarah

Sarah is a head teacher of a small infants' school in a charming country district. A lovely job, you think? In her school she carried a full teaching load as well as all the administrative and management tasks of the head teacher. She found that the various changes imposed by each new education reform threatened to become the straw to break the camel's back.

She had been worried by frequent palpitations, and the doctor had assured her that there was nothing wrong with her heart. Whilst appreciating that cutting out coffee alone would not do anything about the education reforms she decided to see if it would help her feel better. She had also been bothered by weekend headaches and feelings of irritability and lethargy. When she stopped drinking coffee she noticed an immediate benefit, and encouraged her husband to do the same. The headaches did not immediately go away, if anything they were worse for a week or so. But once they were through the withdrawal symptoms they both noticed how much calmer they were. "I stopped running everywhere", she told me, "and my staff commented on how much calmer I was too".

She also found that she slept better. The reason for this is because the stimulating effect of caffeine keeps you awake, and is also a diuretic (it makes you want to pass water a lot). The need to go to the toilet in the night disturbs the normal sleep pattern. Caffeine also has an effect on blood sugar levels causing an inability to concentrate, poor decision making, irritability, nervousness, depression, forgetfulness, hunger and fatigue (all things you can do without when you are under stress). So again, when the effects of the cup of coffee or tea wear off (the blood sugar plummets) there is another reason for the body craving caffeine for a further lift.

Two important stress hormones cortisol and adrenaline are also affected by caffeine. These are the most affected by the flight/fight mechanism. Reducing caffeine intake will also reduce one of the factors triggering the stress response.

Factfile No. 8

Effects of caffeine[2]

Women who drink four to eight cups of tea per day suffered almost five times the pre-menstrual syndrome symptoms of those who drank less.

Women who drank more than one cup of coffee per day (or its equivalent) were only half as likely to get pregnant per menstrual cycle as those who drank less. The effect is thought to be only temporary.

Miscarriage risk was found to be double in women who consumed over 150 mg. of caffeine per day.

High doses of caffeine can produce symptoms totally indistinguishable from anxiety neurosis. If you suffer from anxiety symptoms such as panic attacks or phobias you are advised to remove caffeine entirely from your diet.

Alcohol

We are told that alcohol is good for us. In moderation it helps the body and mind relax, but taken in excess it acts as a depressant, damaging the liver, and impairing brain and sensory function. Some evidence also suggests that moderate alcohol intake reduces cholesterol levels. Many people use alcohol as a way to unwind after a hard day, and socialising with friends over a drink has become an accepted part of Western culture.

The problem is that if you are in a job in which every day is a hard day, alcohol becomes a prop, and props become dependencies. Over a period of time we find we cannot manage without it and damage to our health results, not to mention damage to our relationships, our social lives and our work life.

Excessive alcohol interferes with our sleep patterns and damages the stomach lining, the heart, liver and nervous system. It also causes premature ageing.

Factfile No. 9

Alcohol

For men. You are unlikely to suffer any long-term health problems if you are drinking less that five bottles of wine, 18 pints of beer, or a bottle of spirits a week (or a combination equivalent to one of these limits)

For women. The amount is lower: two bottles of wine, 12 pints of beer, or 4/5 of a bottle of spirits per week. It is better to spread your consumption over the week than to drink it in one or two goes.

Smoking

Increased smoking can result from increased stress. Smokers use tobacco as a prop to help them cope and, as with alcohol, they find they need more and more, and the dependency on the nicotine creates further stress. Nicotine also directly stimulates adrenal glands causing a full stress response.

The damage to health through smoking greatly outweighs any perceived benefits. Smoking affects the lungs, increases the risk of heart disease, chronic bronchitis and emphysema. It is officially recognised that smoking causes cancer, particularly lung cancer. The health of smokers also tends to be generally poorer than other peoples' as smoking affects digestion and therefore absorption of vitamins and essential nutrients.

Stress causes the air passages of the lungs to be dilated and suck in air to their greatest capacity (for flight or fight). Therefore the nicotine and other products of smoking can do the biggest amount of damage to a person under stress. Not only that, just one cigarette can cause the blood vessels, including the coronary arteries, to constrict and heart disease results. Smoking is now known to be the number one preventable health hazard in the world.

In spite of all the evidence available, many people, even nurses and doctors, seem to think that somehow they will be immune. They have a blind spot in this area which technically is known as cognitive dissonance. Cognitive dissonance is caused when something we believe is at odds with something we do. This causes great stress and we have to change either our behaviour or our beliefs in order to reduce this stress. Most smokers find it is easier to rationalise their beliefs than to give up smoking. They say, "It won't happen to me", "I do not believe all that rubbish", "It is my only pleasure", etc., etc.

If you seriously want to help yourself you should begin to note how many cigarettes, cigars or pipes of tobacco you have per day and keep a careful count of this to make sure that you do not allow it to increase in response to daily stresses. Then begin a gradual reduction. There are many ways in which you can be helped to cut out smoking altogether. Some people find that for them cutting out suddenly works best, but getting the motivation to do it is the first step. Next develop a new self-image: stop referring to yourself as a smoker and when you are offered cigarettes do not say, "I'm trying to give up", but to say, "I do not smoke", or "I'm a non-smoker".

To help you kick the habit you will find there are classes available. "When the student is ready the teacher will appear". Once you really make up your mind to do something you find a way to make it possible. Your local Health Education Department (look in the phone book) will be happy to give you details of Smokestop classes, or if you want to go it alone try one of the new nicotine products - gum or patches.

Whichever way you decide, do it in such a way that you do not add hugely to your stress, be gentle with yourself, but appreciate that once you are a non-smoker you will have removed some of the causes of stress in your life - the craving for a cigarettes, and also a factor that is affecting your general health and shortening your life. Find a way to reward yourself on a regular basis.

Tranquillisers

I can not leave this chapter without saying something about tranquillisers and stress, particularly as in the 1980s I made a particular study of them for my Master's Degree. When these drugs were first marketed in the 60s they were hailed as wonder drugs and nicknamed "mother's little helpers". They were thought not to have any side effects, or withdrawal symptoms, and anyone having difficulty in stopping taking them was either labelled as weak, or excessively stressed and therefore still in need of them.

What was not realised until much later is that the benzodiazepine group of drugs, such as diazepam (Valium), cause a chemical addiction, and that the body becomes used to them so a larger and larger dose is needed to create the same effect. Stopping taking them can be hell on earth for long-term users. There are many self-help groups for those who have become dependent on tranquillisers. Short-term use of tranquillisers does have a place for victims of severe trauma and certain psychological illnesses but this is another subject beyond the scope of this book.

Treatments for stress should tackle the underlying stress and not just its symptoms. If you need external help to assist you in coping with the stresses in your life, turn to the chapter on alternative therapies and choose something with no side effects and which will not damage your health.

Serotonin: comfort chemical

Depression, aggression and compulsion have all been shown to correlate with low levels of serotonin which is raised by taking modern anti-depressants such as Prozac. Most people imagine that if a chemical affects human behaviour, its levels have been caused by other chemicals, or by genes. But levels of serotonin in animal and human brains reflect what is happening around them, socially and emotionally. If you are feeling lousy and in need of a drink or a fix or a fling or a fight, you probably have low serotonin levels caused by the way you live.

Studies of animals show that low serotonin is highly sensitive to changes in status in those species where hierarchy is a key organising principle (such as humans). Higher levels of serotonin have been found, for example, in dominant male vervet monkeys, and lower levels in the subordinate ones. But which comes first the high status or the high serotonin levels? In experiments which changed status levels in vervets, serotonin levels tracked the status changes.

Successful human students have been found to have higher serotonin levels. The fact that those who are subordinate or have low status, such as people in low-paid jobs, are more prone to low serotonin problems (depression in women, aggression in men) strongly suggests a link between low serotonin and status.

Factfile No. 10

Serotonin[2]

First identified in the 1940s, serotonin is one of thousands of chemicals found at the places in the brain where physics and chemistry meet, the synapse. The synapse is a gap between the neurones down which electrical impulses pass. When the current reaches the end of a neurone, it causes a chemical reaction in the synapse. Chemical messengers, including serotonin, are despatched and pass the information on to the next neurone, and so on.

Many people unconsciously medicate their low levels using modern drugs of solace. Alcohol raises levels in the short term, lowering them subsequently. MDMA, the key ingredient in Ecstasy, leads to a temporary flooding of serotonin in the short term but, at least in animals, it kills the serotonin receptors, causing permanent damage. Smokers are twice as likely to be depressed, and therefore to be low in serotonin, as non-smokers.

There is still a lot to learn in the field of neurotransmitter research, which includes the study of serotonin. Various ideas are emerging which seem to suggest that the consumption of certain foods including bananas may improve serotonin levels, because neurotransmitters are often made from substances which come from plant foods. Serotonin is made from an amino acid, tryptophan (once sold as a natural anti-depressant) - a naturally occurring amino acid found in bananas and other vegetative materials. High protein foods, such as meat, milk and eggs, can produce feelings of calm because they contain tryptophan, which produces serotonin. Starchy and sugary carbohydrate-rich foods also increase blood sugar and are thought to raise serotonin levels.

However if you are clinically depressed, eating bananas is unlikely to bring about a major benefit, medical help should always be sought. But it is worth remembering that what we eat can often have an effect upon our mood.

"You are what you eat". Changing eating habits is not as difficult as you might think. I became convinced of the importance of a healthy diet when my children were in their teens. Many people say to me, "My family would never eat that!", but I gradually began to introduce wholemeal bread, more nutritious breakfast cereals, more vegetables and less red meat over a period of time. I explained to the family why I was doing it, and the benefits to them. They gradually, if somewhat reluctantly, accepted the changes and now, as adults, they are more enthusiastic even than myself and often reproach me when they come to my home for meals because I do not come up to their own (now) very high dietary standards.

References

1.   Marino, Sal (1997) in *Forbes*, June 2, 1997 v159 n11 p20.

2.   Sigman, Aric *"The Caffeine Trap"*, in *Personnel Management*, July 1990.

3.   James, Oliver (1997) *Britain on the Couch*, Century.

chapter twelve

Movers and shakers

There is no doubt about it, it is official, exercise is good for you. Both for the mind as well as the body. It can improve the quality of your life, and lead to a biochemical change that makes you feel good, as well as improving your physical condition. It has also been found to increase self-esteem, give more restful sleep, build a stronger and more attractive body, and reduce levels of anxiety and depression. More good news is that exercise reduces the effects of ageing, and increases energy.

Maureen

Maureen closed her office door and leaned against it for a moment, before crossing the office to sink wearily down at her desk. It had been a difficult meeting, one for which she had been unprepared. She drew the back of her hand across her forehead and leaned her head on her hand. She had needed all of her stress management skills to keep her cool (thank goodness for breathing exercises!) and some good communication skills to get her point across. That manager from Section B had been particularly difficult this afternoon. Maureen still hadn't found a way of responding resourcefully to his constant criticisms of her department. "What is it with him?" she wondered. "Is it because I'm a woman, or because I'm new to the company? I suppose it could even be because I've got a degree and he's worked his way up."

Since taking on this role six months ago Maureen had begun to realise that she had a lot of learning to do in order to fit her for this new management role. She found meetings particularly difficult. Being the new girl around here and very aware of the fact, she would need to prove herself before they would listen to her ideas. But it was important that she convince the rest of the management team of the validity of her suggestions, otherwise her department would not get much share of this year's budget for the new projects they hoped to undertake.

She had a hard-working but difficult team, fiercely loyal to their previous manager who had been moved on to another branch of the company. They rather resented Maureen's presence. She had returned to the work environment after a career break only two years ago and had been finding it hard to move back to the level of seniority she had had before starting her family. This job was her first opportunity to show that she had not lost her old abilities, but she was very aware that her confidence and her self-assurance were still vulnerable. Whilst being a housewife and mother, the only meetings she'd attended were family conferences. "They must wonder if I am up to it", she thought, and knew she put added pressure on herself with this thought. She also wondered how much her insecurities showed.

Maureen was very grateful to have obtained this post, at this time. An added blow had been her recent divorce. She was having to come to terms with the pain of it all, as well as the new job, and the financial challenge of supporting herself and two children.

She straightened her shoulders and smiled. "I won't give in, or let this spoil my evening", she said to herself. In a few moments she would gather up her papers and prepare for home, taking with her some figures which she needed to work on for the following day, the first batch of which she'd begin immediately after tea.

The rest of the figures she would leave until later because she had promised Anne a game of badminton. Anne was her best friend, and also divorced. Their weekly game of badminton coupled with the swimming sessions later in the week were a life-saver for both of them. Since taking this job Maureen found she needed the physical activity to burn off the tension of the day. She knew that it helped her regain her equilibrium. She'd found exercise very useful many years before when she was a student taking her final exams. Then it had been regular games of tennis with her flat mate. She had quite forgotten how energised she used to feel after the exercise, and how the feeling lasted, enabling her to survive the exam pressure.

She felt sure that the energy she was able to put into solving the many problems she had encountered since starting this job was due at least in part to the increased physical stamina she had developed through her present exercise routine.

Even so, she often found it hard to motivate herself to get out of the house on exercise nights. When it was cold and wet with the rain rattling against the window-panes it would have been so easy to put Anne off and curl up in front of the TV instead. She knew Anne felt the same, but neither wanted to be the one to "chicken-out". So they usually managed to encourage each other and arrive at the Sports Complex glad for each others' support.

A tap sounded at the office door bringing Maureen quickly back to earth. It was Leslie handing in the keys to the offices at the bottom end of the building before going home. "Thank you, Leslie, Good night." She took the keys and placed them ready for the cleaners who would be along later, and turned to gather up her papers.

Research being conducted at the University of Nebraska[1] is beginning to suggest that people who participate in regular physical training demonstrate an increased biochemical challenge response when they are exposed to non-physical stressors such as a puzzle or exam. The training toughens up the person by boosting the chemical reaction which produces this response, so that under stress you will be far tougher than someone who has not exercised. But the training must be short and not too strong to produce this toughening effect, and must be balanced by periods of recovery in between. Too rigorous or too long training can tip the scales, and instead of being an athlete you will become an over-trained burnout victim. In everyday life this translates to work hard but play hard.

Like a finely tuned sports car, a fit person has the body machinery to marshal all the physical systems needed to quickly go from zero to 60, and just as quickly put on the brakes when it is no longer needed. People who are not fit, on the other hand, take far longer to warm up into action, are far less efficient when they finally do get going, and take far longer to cool down.

Responding to stress is similar. People who have a good stress response are not those who experience little or no stress reaction. Rather, they are people who can marshal the appropriate biochemistry to deal with the stress at a moment's notice, creating a big boost of helpful hormones for the task in hand, and then just as quickly turn it off.

Factfile No. 11

Exercise

Exercise can:

enhance mood, relieve depression and anxiety thus regulating emotions

produce a state of relaxation through reduction of physiological tension

neutralise stress

increase glucose production and therefore a steady flow of energy

strengthen immunity

reduce the risk of brittle bone disease

improve circulation, and flow of oxygen to the cells

maintain elasticity of the arteries

help balance cholesterol

improve blood pressure

lessen the risk of heart disease

reduce the affects of ageing

tone respiratory system, increasing exchanges of oxygen and carbon dioxide

help the body eliminate metabolic wastes

promote sounder sleep

However exercise does not eliminate or change the stressor (it is not problem-focused) but it can be an emotional regulator (emotion-focused), and dealing with your emotional responses may be necessary before you can deal with the problem itself. In helping you deal with stress, exercise has been found to be just as helpful as using intellectual strategies[2]. So a regular exercise regime can help you become more stress-proof, and can be part of your overall coping repertoire, making you feel better about yourself. But the optimum word is regular. The benefits of exercise will only be felt when it is properly planned and regularly taken.

If you have experienced positive mood changes, noticed how your tension is reduced, or developed a new way of thinking about a problem as a result of exercise, you are likely to have developed confidence to know that when something bad happens you can change the way you feel and the way to act towards it. You will realise that these things too are under your control.

With all these benefits to be obtained from exercise why is it that some people find it so difficult to make the effort? There are people for whom the mere thought of exercise brings a shudder. The answer could be that people do not think carefully enough about what would suit them, and fit into their lifestyle. Many people undertake exercise regimes that are unrealistic, time-consuming, expensive and generally not something that they really want to do. They make it another of life's oughts. To succeed it has to be the right exercise for you, the kind of exercise that you enjoy as well as need. The activity should suit your personality, your timetable, and your physical capabilities. Forcing yourself into an exercise routine that you do not enjoy would do little for your motivation and you would probably give up. Exercise should give you pleasure as well as do you good.

Begin gently, not pushing yourself too hard, and if you have a health problem it might be advisable to check with your doctor about which type of exercise you can safely undertake. Little and often is better than a major work out less frequently. Sudden activity in someone not used to it can block the flow of blood to the heart and increase the risk of a heart attack. So a medical check-up before beginning a fitness programme is also a good idea. But if you are moderately and sensibly active your risk is minimal.

On completion of any exercise routine you should feel good. If you do not sleep well or are tired and aching the next day you may have done too much, or not warmed up properly before exercising. It is important to start with little and often. To help you decide let us look at some different forms of exercise and what people have said about them.

It has been said[3] that the best antidote to stress is aerobic exercise. This works by increasing your body's consumption of oxygen, raising your heart rate and making your arteries and lungs expand. Aerobic exercise uses the large muscle groups in a repetitive fashion, forcing you to breathe deeply on a consistent basis. It should be continued for 20 to 30 minutes resulting in increased fitness. Jogging, brisk walking, aerobic dancing, cycling, swimming and vigorous racquet games are all aerobic exercises. So an alternative to lonely jogging in the early morning, could be to join a squash or badminton club and exercise with friends.

Walking is something we could find natural opportunities to do without needing to spend any money, or join any clubs, and if done correctly it can provide aerobic exercise. Andrew Weil[4] pares all his comments and advice on exercise down to one word: "Walk!" He believes that walking is the most healthful form of physical activity. You do not have to learn how to do it. It does not require any equipment except a comfortable pair of shoes.

It costs nothing, and you can do it almost anywhere. The chance of injuring yourself is small, in great contrast to running and competitive sports. It is much less boring than riding an exercise bicycle or working a treadmill. You can walk outdoors and enjoy the beauty of nature. You can also walk with friends and enjoy their company.

Weil comments on the fact that in non-industrial societies the demands of daily life give bodies all the work they need. People lift and carry burdens, and they walk constantly, giving their muscles good tone. They walk to gather water and wood, they walk to their fields, they walk to markets, and they walk to visit friends and relatives. Of all the technological inventions that have changed our patterns of activity for the worse, he gives the automobile first prize, not just because it has compromised health significantly due to exhaust emissions, but because it has deprived us of opportunities to walk. We therefore need to incorporate walking more consciously into our daily lives, if we live in towns and cities, or work in less active jobs.

Walking will satisfy all the body's needs for aerobic exercise if it is done in ways that increase the heart rate and respiration sufficiently. For an ideal aerobic workout, your walks should last 45 minutes, and you should be able to cover three miles in that time. If your heart and respiratory rate are not elevated at the end of a 45 minute walk, you should try walking faster part of the time or look for long, gradual hills to climb.

Useful advice on choosing suitable exercise is also given in *The Book of Stress Survival*[6]. Its author, Alix Kirsta, also gives the following chart which might help you choose a suitable activity.

Factfile No 12
Different types of exercise and its benefits
Aerobic dance

Key facts

How it works: Combines dance steps, callisthenics, running in place, hopping, and jumping, all set to music; borrows from many different types of dance.

What you need: Shorts and T-shirt or leotard and tights, comfortable and not too tight fitting. A space about 9 x 12 ft (3 x 4m.), plus an instruction book and record or a video cassette. Or you can join a class.

Time required: Classes usually run for 1 hour twice a week.

Body confidence

Exercising to music and learning routines can lift the spirits and boost confidence. You can expect improvements in balance, stride, posture and body image.

Recommended:
If you think you are unathletic, artistic, or musical. Classes appeal if you are sociable and like working with a teacher.
Note. Avoid if you have disorder of the foot, knee, back, or ankle.

Fitness benefits

Flexibility: A good programme will increase flexibility through 10-20 mins of warm up and stretching exercises.

Strength: Abdominal muscles are strengthened by sit-ups and leg raises, legs with running and kicks. There are usually no exercises to increase upper-body strength.

Cardiovascular endurance: Classes usually include 20-30 mins. continuous jumping, dancing, and jogging for cardiovascular endurance.

Aerobic exercise

Key facts

How it works: Sustained running, fast walking, swimming, or cycling increases your consumption of oxygen, raising your heart rate, and expanding your lungs and arteries. Done regularly, this form of exercise speeds up the metabolism and the rate at which you burn up calories, even when at rest.

What you need: A track suit, shorts, and sweat shirt, and training shoes for running.

Time required: 10-20 mins. daily.

Body confidence

Increased endurance and strength offer good benefits here. Testing your personal best by recording distances and timings and extending your limits improves self-image.

Recommended:

If you like simple exercises that you can do outdoors and that take only a short time; if you like exercising alone; if your competitive spirit is low.

Note: Avoid if you have a physical weakness or injury.

Fitness benefits

Flexibility: Do 5 mins. stretching and flexing exercises before and after running to avoid injury and promote flexibility. Cycling and swimming improve muscle flexibility.

Strength: Excellent improvements are possible, especially in the strength of the legs and hips.

Cardiovascular endurance: Aerobic exercise is second to none in strengthening your heart and lungs and improving overall stamina.

Callisthenics

Key facts

How it works: Uses general keep-fit exercises that stretch and tone the muscles without using equipment. They are useful on their own or before sports.

What you need: Leotard and tights, a track suit, or shorts and T-shirt. Beginners should consider joining a class, although a book of exercises can start you off, or keep you going later.

Time required: A 30-40 min session, preferably daily. Pre-sport callisthenics take 10-20 mins.

Body confidence

Stretching and toning of the muscles improves alignment, posture and stride.

Recommended:

If you are self-disciplined and like to exercise on your own; if you are on a rigid schedule, since you can do callisthenics anywhere; if you like mechanical, non-taxing exercise.

Fitness benefits

Flexibility: Stretching callisthenics exercises can greatly improve all-over flexibility.

Strength: Callisthenics build your strength, although not as quickly as using weights.

Cardiovascular endurance: If supplemented with programme of running or jumping rope, callisthenics can improve cardiovascular endurance.

Yoga

Key facts

How it works: Uses postures, held for a sustained period, for attaining mental and physical balance and well-being.

What you need: Loose comfortable clothing or leotard and tights. Classes are given by experienced teachers. Once you have learned the basics, a book of yoga exercises will help you.

Time required: A yoga session should last at least 30 mins, and be done at least three times a week. Classes last 1-1.5 hrs.

Body confidence

Yoga emphasises body awareness and so encourages physical self-respect; it helps you to become more aware of body function and posture.

Recommended:

If you have problems with muscular tension; if you lead a pressured, highly stressed life; if you want exercise for the mind as well as the body; if you cannot do vigorous physical activity; if you are patient.

Fitness benefits

Flexibility: One of the main aims of yoga is to improve flexibility by stretching and toning all parts of the body.

Strength: Holding postures increase muscle strength only minimally. Some programmes also include strength exercises to make up for this lack.

Cardiovascular endurance: Yoga does little for cardiovascular endurance.

Weight machines

Key facts

How it works: The machines hold the weights and you work the movable parts. There are machines for nearly every muscle group.

What you need: Access to a set of weight machines. This means joining a health club or gym. Wear a sweat suit or shorts, T-shirt and sneakers.

Time required: About 30 mins three times a week. Longer or more frequent work-outs are counterproductive because of muscle fatigue.

Body confidence

Seeing steady improvements in the amount of weight you can lift is rewarding.

Recommended:

If you want visible results quickly; if you like indoor exercise in a club atmosphere with the advantage of working alone; if you can afford club fees.

Fitness benefits

Flexibility: This improves if you use the machines correctly, extending the muscles fully before each move.

Strength: This is the main benefit of using weight machines.

Cardiovascular endurance: The gain here is minimal. Add some jogging, cycling, or swimming if you want an improvement in cardiovascular endurance.

Martial arts

Key facts

How it works: These forms of eastern self-defence training teach a range of manoeuvres - kicks, punches, and holds. T'ai chi is slower and dance like.

What you need: An outfit called a gi, consisting of pants, jacket and belt. For t'ai chi, loose fitting clothing and comfortable shoes. You must attend a class.

Time required: Classes take 1 - 2 hours and should be taken at least twice a week for several years.

Body confidence

A major benefit. The martial arts promote physical and emotional self-awareness and foster self-defence expertise.

Recommended:

If you are adventurous and prepared for the long-term commitment required; if you want a discipline that involves a lot of body contact and physicality; if you want to develop your self-defence capability.

Fitness benefits

Flexibility: Most programmes include stretching exercises, aiding the flexibility required for high kicks and other movements.

Strength: Karate and judo usually incorporate strength-building exercises including push-ups and sit-ups.

Cardiovascular endurance: Most types (except t'ai chi) spend a lot of time on routines that exercise the heart.

Laughter is also a form of exercise and one which we often do not use nearly enough. Children laugh, on average, 500 times in a day. Adults laugh, on average, 14 in a day. I wonder why this should be? Learning to laugh more often can help us relax and also can promote a powerful physiological reaction which makes us more stress-proof and more healthy. Laughter should become one of our stress-proofing skills, and stress-handling skills. Hearty laughter can move us into a state of high positive energy, a state of fun when we are at our most creative.

Factfile No 13

The physiology of laughter

When we laugh we lose muscle control and relax

Our diaphragm convulses and gets a much needed workout

Our internal organs get massaged, helping internal circulation

The cardiovascular system dilates

Initially blood pressure rises significantly but after we stop it returns to a lower resting rate than normal

The circulatory system is exercised through constricting and dilating, and becomes more flexible

A high amount of oxygen is inhaled and we can oxygenate muscles and brain

Respiratory system is getting a workout

Our faces move up and down and this relaxes the thymus gland which shrinks when we are under stress. The thymus is important in the immune system, responsible for producing lymphocytes containing T-cells which attack cancer cells we produce daily

The brain releases endorphin which is a morphine-like neuropeptide which is a powerful natural pain killer, and also cortisol, which is an anti-inflammatory

---

Laughter costs nothing and is freely available yet we take on, without questioning, three core myths about laughter which are endemic in our culture.

1. That you need a reason to laugh. So we monitor our reasons for laughing and keep a check on our humour. If we laugh without reason people ask us, "What is there to laugh about?"

2. You have to be happy to laugh. Untrue. We do not laugh because we are happy, we are happy because we laugh. Laughter releases the stress and tension which build up when we are unhappy. Laughter can often lead to us taking a fresh look at our difficulties and finding an appropriate way out of them

3. A sense of humour and laughter are the same thing - they are not. You do not need a sense of humour to laugh. Laughter is innate and spontaneous. A sense of humour is culturally dependent and is learnt.

If everyone else around you is being very serious it takes courage to laugh. You may be challenged. There is a mistaken belief that we should not laugh when we are unhappy. Some of the most highly-stressed professions, police, fire service, ambulance for example, have a strong culture of humour under difficult circumstances. I believe it is done instinctively in order to make a difficult situation controllable and to reduce stress levels. This is important because when stress levels are high, mistakes are made and in that kind of a job you cannot afford to make mistakes. Laughter also develops the team spirit which is so necessary for working together.

But beware of gallows humour. Gallows humour is sick humour, and has been described as "an effort by the powerless to make the tolerable more bearable". This is forced laugher. Nor should it be laughter at the expense of others. This puts other people down and creates more pain and tension, as does putting oneself down. Healthy laughter should leave you and others feeling physically, emotionally and mentally better.

Laughter has beneficial mental effects. It helps us get a sense of perspective on our problems and keeps our mind engaged in the present. We can find ourselves much better able to generate creative and effective solutions to problems. Laughter can play a part in your personal development. It can increase a sense of alignment and congruence. It provides a natural and effective way to become aware of the gap between who we really are and the image we present to the world. Laughter can reduce this gap. Laughter really is good medicine. Try to see the funny side of situations and do not take everything so seriously. Have you ever noticed how laughter can suddenly break an attack of anger? A good giggle can be a healthy release from tension, stress, embarrassment and lethargy. Some tips for developing more laughter which Mariana Funes[6] recommends:

1. Find out how you stop yourself laughing. Notice when you buy into the laughter myths and when you catch yourself doing it. Laugh for a full minute for no reason at all!

2. Share your embarrassing moments. Do this in a factual way (just describing what happened) without putting yourself or others down.

3. Keep a diary of what makes you laugh.

4. Find something very serious in your life and tell yourself repeatedly how very serious it really is!

5. Fake it until you make it. If you just do not think it is funny, pretend. Your diaphragm cannot tell the difference between real laughter and a fake, as you fake it the real one will kick-in.

6. And finally when all else fails, you can always say tee-hee. Seriously, add a simple tee-hee to whatever you take most seriously ...if tee-hee does not work, ho-ho or ha-ha may well do the job!

Remember the words of Arthur Koestler: "Ha-ha can lead to ah-ha!"

No matter how much activity you take, or how much laughing you do, it must be balanced by rest. A lack of good quality sleep affects the immune system. Improving the quality of rest and sleep should be another priority in your stress-management programme and the next chapter will give you some ideas if insomnia is a problem.

References

1. Dientsbier, University of Nebraska, quoted in *Second Opinion: stress for success,* (psychological stress) Forbes FYI March 13, 1995 v.155 n6 pS67(3).

2. Long BC and Flood K R "Coping with work stress: psychological benefits of exercise", *Work and Stress*, 1993, 7, No. 2, 109-119.

3. Long , B C 1993a, "Aerobic conditioning(jogging) and stress inoculation interventions: an exploratory study of coping", *International Journal of Sport Psychology*, 24, 26-40.

4. Weil, Andrew (1995) *Spontaneous Healing*, Warner Books, London.

5. Kirsta, Alix (1986) *The Book of Stress Survival*, Unwin Paperbacks, London.

6. Funes, Dr. Marian, "Plerking Around", in *Management Skills and Development*, September 1997.

chapter thirteen

Not waving but drowning

Just as the young people in South Africa sometimes found they needed the help of a friend when the strength or unexpectedness of a wave had knocked them off their feet and they were in danger of being swamped, so we too sometimes need external help to survive life's stresses. Even when we are managing very well, professional assistance to reduce the amount of tension and improve our physical health can be very beneficial. This helps us keep "on our feet" to face the waves of stress as they come. Asking for help from an external source is therefore a sensible step in the restabilising process. Anyone in a highly pressured job, or with stressful life circumstances, should know where they can turn for some help and this help is often found through what is known as alternative medicine or complementary therapy. In recent years this has become increasingly popular in the UK, and is already well established in Australia and in the States. Many of these therapies are finding favour with mainstream medical practitioners and being recommended by GPs.

There are a wide range of therapists, counsellors and professional helpers available, and finding one that is right for you can sometimes be quite difficult. In this chapter I have tried to highlight some of the therapies found to be most beneficial in treating stress related conditions, and give some information about each which should help you to decide which might be most helpful to yourself.

Marion

It was two o'clock and Gina hadn't returned from her lunch yet. Marion looked at her empty desk and consciously chose not to react. Six months ago she would have felt the feelings of anger and frustration rise within her when yet another lunch break was over and Gina was not back at her desk. It wasn't difficult to know where she was, or whom she was with, but what to do about it, that was a different matter. For nine months now Gina had been having an affair with Marion's immediate boss, both of them already married. Marion had no idea how many people knew about this. She herself had confronted her boss with her own knowledge and had been told to mind her own business, in no uncertain terms. He had even suggested that if she didn't like the situation she might like to consider finding another job. Being in a rather specialised field of work Marion was terrified that she would never find another job at this level within travelling distance of home. She needed to continue to live in the area because of her husband's job and children's schools. So she kept quiet, and fumed inwardly.

Eventually, the anger she felt, and the pent-up frustration of having to allow Gina to do substandard work, began to eat away at her. She spent most of her evenings in tears, headachy, no appetite, going over and over the situation in her own mind, and with her husband. Inevitably she became so ill she was unable to work, and her GP signed her off. "Now Gina will have to pull her weight," she thought.

Marion had begun to contemplate returning to work. After two months off sick she was feeling better, but knowing that the situation was no different she dreaded facing everything again. Prior to her return she attended a stress-management course which I was conducting. As part of the course she completed a stress-management questionnaire and her own score was so high I had a private chat with her during the lunch break. I learned the above details and I counselled Marion to seek some external help in the form of counselling. I also suggested taking more exercise and improving her diet, together with a range of other coping strategies.

Marion took my advice and when I saw her six months later she was a different person. She had a spring in her step and a sparkle in her eye. The situation was still the same but she was coping differently. She already had a good exercise routine, and had taken my advice about diet, but more than anything she found the help of a counsellor was most beneficial in helping her get things into perspective.

She told me, "One of the things I learned was that I was transferring feelings which rightly belonged to my own father onto my boss. You see, when I was small my father was always cheating on my mother, and my mother used to pretend it wasn't happening, and put up with it for our sakes. We all knew what was going on, we had seen him with the other woman, and hated him for making our mother so miserable. As I child I raged inwardly at his treatment of her but was powerless to do anything about it. Whenever I tried to say anything the grown-ups used to hush me up. The counsellor helped me to recognise that this was the real source of my anger, and that I could separate these feelings from the feelings I had about my boss and Gina. When I did that I got it into perspective. I knew that my responsibility towards Gina was simply making sure that she did her job. I didn't have to be responsible for her morals, any more than I was responsible for those of my boss. What a relief it was. I was able to go back to work and carry on with my job. Providing that work is not affected I now believe that what goes on between Gina and my boss is their problem and the consequences are their responsibility. But I shall be actively looking for another job."

In looking for another job Marion was making plans to get away from the stress but only after she had developed her inner resources to cope, so that she would be leaving with positive feelings and improved self-esteem. If she had just taken the easy way out and found another job she might have walked into another difficult situation and gone through similar agonies.

She told me that one of the things that had made her take action was the fact that I, who had never met her before, had cautioned her about the extent of her stress and how it was affecting her. Until that point she had just been hoping that it would all go away. In sessions with her counsellor she discovered the value of not only a listening ear, but a professional one, who knew how to listen, and also knew which questions to ask and how to ask them, so that Marion herself started to find her way out of the anguish she was suffering.

That is part of what counselling is about. There are many forms of counselling and psychological help which are invaluable when problems become so great they are interfering with normal life, and the stigmas associated with seeking this kind of help are fortunately disappearing. Not only that, but as more and more employers become aware of the loss of productivity which results when employees are stressed, whether the stress is personal or work-related, many companies are employing their own in-house counsellors or to use the American terminology Employee Assistance Programmes. Other companies are contracting with outside agencies to provide help. You could find out if one is available through your organisation before you pay to see someone privately. You may also be able to access the services of a counsellor through your doctor. In the UK this is likely to be a free service but may well have a time limit of, say, six or ten weeks.

If you decide to find a private counsellor do not just choose one out of the paper. In fact do not do that with any form of therapy. Always get a list of qualified and reputable practitioners from a professional body, you will find lists of agencies in the appendix. Another good method of finding someone is by personal recommendation. At the end of the day it often boils down to finding someone you feel comfortable with, and believe you can trust. Have an initial meeting with them and only continue with consultations if you feel that this person is right for you.

Counselling help is also available from other sources. As an alternative to counselling, your GP might suggest seeing a psychologist, or a psychotherapist. Neither of these are necessarily doctors although some may have dual qualifications, and are not to be confused with psychiatrists. Psychiatrists are medical doctors who are also highly specialised in illnesses of the mind. Their role is to make a diagnosis and prescribe treatment. People are usually referred to a psychiatrist when their problem has become so great that it is interfering with their normal life. Some psychiatrists also practise psychotherapy and will spend time helping you to understand the source of your problems, but within the National Health Service time does not often allow this. Psychologists on the other hand are specialists in the field of human understanding. They are not doctors of medicine although many of them have doctorates in other subjects. Referral to a psychologist does not mean that your doctor thinks you are suffering from mental illness.

There are other health professionals who often possess counselling skills, and they include social workers, nurses and occupational therapists. If you come into contact with one of them you may find that some counselling sessions are part of your therapy. You might also find others who use counselling and helping skills as part of their job without necessarily being trained counsellors. They include teachers, managers, supervisors, clergy, church workers, doctors, trade union workers, and also financial and legal advisors such as solicitors.

All of us have the opportunity to assist others, be it in the role of marital partner, parent, relative, friend or workmate. You may be fortunate to find that you have someone with a good listening ear amongst your acquaintances and in the first instance their help might enable you to begin to get things into perspective.

Counselling fosters a relationship which involves a repertoire of skills and is a process which begins with two people, and ideally ends as a self-help process as the counsellee works his or her way through problems and begins to work out solutions with greater clarity of thought. It emphasises self-help and individual choice. At the end of the period of counselling the counsellee should feel better able to make decisions and work his or her way out of their difficulties.

Counselling is not the only form of help available for emotional difficulties. Many people find that techniques to help them calm their mind and relax their body are what they need to help them switch off the stress response. Some people find this help through learning meditation techniques. Meditation is a very ancient mental discipline which is included in the practice of many world religions including Christianity, Judaism, Islam, Buddhism and Hinduism and within these religions it is practised as a form of spiritual enlightenment. However in the West it is used widely in a non-religious context and you need not fear being coerced into joining one of the Eastern religions. It needs to be practised regularly and you learn to induce a state of deep rest in mind and body by withdrawing from external reality and achieving deep relaxation and increased mental clarity, usually using some form of attention focus to which the mind can return if distracted. This may be a breathing pattern, a physical object, a repetitive movement, or a word. In meditation the brainwaves change to a distinctive alpha pattern linked with deep relaxation and mental alertness. Meditation has been shown to reverse the body's flight/fight response and is therefore valuable in treating stress-related conditions, insomnia, migraine, blood pressure problems, asthma, angina and drug dependency, and there are no side effects.

States of deep relaxation may be achieved in other ways. Flotation therapy is quite a popular way of using a state of sensory deprivation in which deep relaxation is achieved. It is said to be a short cut to meditation, and it is claimed that 40 minutes flotation is equal to six hours of sleep. (I could see this being very valuable to insomniacs who are getting desperate.) It is a therapy developed in the US during the 1970s. Treatment involves lying in an enclosed and sound-proofed bath or small room, with sufficient salts and minerals dissolved in the water to enable the body to float effortlessly. Total sensory deprivation is the aim but many people find they want at least one of their senses engaged, particularly the first time. So whilst flotation takes place in complete or semi-darkness, floaters can at any time switch on a light or open the door. It is also possible to have music playing whilst floating, and most centres will allow you to take along your own tapes or CDs. Sessions last one to one and a half hours and may be repeated as often as you like. During flotation the mind and body enter a profound state of relaxation. The brain releases endorphins and subjects experience a state of mild euphoria. In this state the mind becomes very receptive to suggestion and daydreaming, not unlike that state you would achieve under hypnotherapy.

Hypnotherapy is another form of treatment which you may find helpful. Some people have fears about it because they are afraid of losing control and are worried about being unduly influenced by the hypnosis, particularly if they have watched any of the stage hypnotist shows. But you need to appreciate that there is a great difference between a person who uses hypnotism as a form of entertainment and a reputable hypnotherapist. A hypnotherapist simply guides the subject into an altered state of consciousness, similar to daydreaming. In this trance-like state the subject is open to suggestions which can influence the mind and body in ways which would not be possible ordinarily. It has been called relaxed awareness. The subject then learns to recreate this state on their own. A good hypnotherapist can help promote relaxation, control pain and overcome bad habits, such as smoking, as well as helping subjects deal with a range of other problems. Again, it is very important to find a therapist you can trust and feel comfortable with, as this is vital in achieving an altered state of consciousness.

Hypnotherapy has moved away from earlier associations with quackery and has gained respect within the medical establishment. I myself know several doctors who have learned to practise hypnotherapy with great skills, but they are often regarded with some scepticism by their colleagues.

Another of the Eastern disciplines which has been introduced into the West and has achieved great popularity is yoga. The system originated over 5,000 years ago in India where it is traditionally practised by Hindu ascetics. Like meditation it was originally a preparation for spiritual development. In the West it has grown in popularity in the last 50 years along with many other Eastern disciplines which promote well-being, and, no, you do not have to lie on a bed of nails! You may have become aware of it as a form of gentle exercise consisting of body postures and breathing techniques. It is in fact a complete system of mental and physical training. Its aim is to unite physical, mental and spiritual health, which is what the word yoga means – union. It induces spiritual awareness, deep relaxation, mental tranquillity, concentration and clarity, fused with physical strength and suppleness. Its coordinated system of breathing relaxes mind and body, stimulates circulation, and increases the supply of oxygen to all the tissues. Relaxation of both body and mind is vital to yoga, making it a good way of banishing tension. It is unique because it not only stretches the body but also massages the internal organs and glands. A friend who recently began yoga classes for the first time told me that she felt as if she had had a gentle massage when she came away from the class. These classes are often run in local schools or adult education centres for a modest fee, and your local library may have details.

Massage in any form is an excellent way of relieving tension and strain. For years beauty salons have offered facial and neck and shoulder massage to stressed female executives, who have recognised how helpful his can be. Nowadays you do not have to be a stressed female executive but the beauty parlour might be the place to start. However massage also has a place outside the beauty parlour and is considered to be a valuable form of therapy for males and females.

There are many forms of massage available and, whilst the word massage still conjures up the nudge, nudge, wink, wink reaction, there are many genuine massage practitioners who can be found in directories of alternative therapists, offering a service designed to relax and re-invigorate you. A session with a masseuse who will work on your muscles to release tension, and stimulate circulation, simultaneously releasing toxins which stress has built up in your tissues, can produce enormous feelings of well-being. Massage has been practised in the East for centuries and it is one of the oldest forms of therapy. The Chinese and Japanese have long understood the value of working on the body in this way. Acceptance of various forms of massage is at last finding its way into Western culture.

There are many good books on massage available in book stores, and with a partner you could learn to massage each other. Whilst genuine massage should be divorced from sexual connotations you might also find that this increased physical contact with your sexual partner enriches your love life. It is also possible to attend short courses on massage, but as it is so difficult to give oneself a complete massage it would probably be a good idea to attend with a partner. Go with your best friend, if your partner is not interested, and learn to massage each other.

Variations of massage have developed in the West over many years. For example there is remedial massage, manual lymph drainage, and biodynamic massage to name but three. Each form of massage has its own special purpose, but generally the aim is to ease away muscular tension, to dispel tiredness, and to reinforce depleted or unbalanced energy. It has the added benefit of helping you to prevent future physical weaknesses and strains. The maseur or masseuse can identify prime tension spots, commonly found on the neck, shoulders and back, and fibrositic nodules of tissue. By stroking, rubbing, kneading, pulling and hacking movements these tense tight muscles can be helped to relax, and circulation improved by elimination of toxic waste. During massage you become aware of the most subtle feelings of pleasure and discomfort. At an emotional level a good massage can soothe stress and tension, create feelings of well-being and enhance self-esteem.

Eastern massage includes acupressure techniques such as shiatsu. Acupressure itself has been described as acupuncture without needles but is probably much earlier in origin. Acupuncture is a traditional Chinese medicine and its unique feature is the insertion of needles into particular parts of the body. It is used to manipulate the energy flows around the body via meridians or energy lines, and its primary purpose is not to destress or change behaviour, but to restore and maintain health and to prevent illness. Stimulation of the many acupuncture points all over the body can also strengthen or relax the internal organs, the spine, and the central nervous system. A side effect of this could well be the release of tension.

In acupressure, however, finger pressure is used instead of needles. For centuries it has been used to treat aches and pains, overcome tiredness, and reduce tension. Nervous tension and stress-related disorder can be treated by sedating specific points on the energy lines.

Shiatsu is a form of body work, or massage, which was developed in Japan early in the 20th century. It follows the same principles and meridians as acupressure, and the practitioner uses firm pressure from fingers, thumbs, elbows, knees, even feet, in a combination of massage techniques. It is intended to increase the circulation of vital energy. Western practitioners claim that it regulates the hormonal system and the circulation of the blood and lymphatic fluid, aids the elimination of waste products and releases muscle tension. It is believed to work as a general tonic and also enhance the body's self-healing abilities. I have found it a valuable destressor and I have been told that after a shiatsu session I "look like a page that hasn't been written on".

Aromatherapists also use massage as a way of rubbing essential oils into the tissues. The oils used are distilled from the essence of fruits, plants and herbs which have specific curative and restorative properties and combine the medicinal properties of these plants with the tradition of a healing massage. The oils can also be added to bath water, allowing their fragrance to be released through the steam. Their action on the mind and body is subtle and profound. When inhaled, they act on the brain and nervous system via the stimulus of the olfactory nerves, helping to alter mood, dispel fatigue or irritability, and alleviate depression or anxiety. There is also some evidence that they may be partly absorbed through the skin, allowing more powerful, active constituents to be released into the tissues and the bloodstream. The scents released by the oils are believed to act on the hypothalamus, the part of the brain influencing the hormone system, and are thought to affect libido, mood, metabolism, and stress levels.

Modern aromatherapy practice is largely based on research by doctors in France, where essential oils are sometimes prescribed as alternatives to conventional medicine. Outside France aromatherapy initially became popular as a beauty treatment, and cheaper, less potent versions of genuine aromatherapy oils are available over the counter and via mail order. Whilst these will add a pleasant perfume to a home massage, they are not to be confused with the real thing. Genuine oils are prescribed by a qualified aromatherapist and can also be bought over the counter, but look for the label "pure essential oil" and make sure that the oils aren't mixed with any other medium. Be aware also that quality may vary.

Massage is also included in the treatment offered by reflexologists although in this instance it is likely to be confined to the feet and ankles, occasionally the hands and arms. Often reflexology and aromatherapy are used in conjunction with each other. Like acupressure, reflexology works by applying pressure. It is deeply relaxing and consists of deep, steady pressing and rolling movements made using the edge of the thumb. The object is to induce relaxation, improve energy, restore healthy circulation and eliminate toxins. The theory is that there are points on the soles of the feet which correspond to the various parts of the body and by massaging and applying pressure to these points the therapist can stimulate the body's own natural healing processes. This has also been known to be a valuable diagnostic tool, highlighting problem areas. It is said to work best for disorders of the internal organs and for stress-related symptoms, such as headaches, constipation and tension.

Another therapy promoting healing from within is chiropractic. As a result of its success in treating back problems, headaches, and sports and other injuries, it is the most widely practised branch of complementary medicine in the West. It has been well-researched and medical opinion is generally well-disposed towards this form of treatment. It is a form of spinal manipulation which was invented a century ago by Daniel D Palmer, a Canadian. He tested his theories by manipulating the spine of his office janitor, who had been deaf for 17 years after a back and neck injury. This allegedly caused a click and the janitor's hearing returned. Head and neck pain, shoulder stiffness, back problems, poor sleep pattern and a range of other conditions can be caused or exacerbated by spinal misalignment and the chiropractor works to bring the bones of the skeleton into correct alignment. Chiropractic treatment can be helpful in cases of acute musculo-skeletal pain, tension headaches, and recovery from trauma but is less effective if the pain is chronic. A twice-yearly visit to a chiropractor is well worth while and is recommended as a health investment.

There are some variations of chiropractic which were developed in the 20th century by two British chiropractors, known as the McTimoney and McTimoney-Corley chiropractic. These use gentle uncomplicated forms of adjustment and practitioners focus on the whole body at each session, as they believe that the body needs to be completely realigned each time. The gentleness of these techniques makes them relatively comfortable to receive, and they are therefore particularly recommended for babies and the elderly.

Chiropractic has much in common with osteopathy but is an entirely different discipline. Osteopathy was developed in the USA in the late 19th century. The aim of this approach to diagnosis and treatment of musculo-skeletal disorders is to restore or improve mobility and balance by use of massage and manipulation. Osteopaths have official recognition as doctors in the USA, and osteopathy is finding increasing acceptance among health professionals elsewhere. Whereas chiropractors often concentrate on manipulation of misaligned joints, osteopaths may focus on soft tissue treatment to relax muscles and bring back joint mobility.

By developing correct alignment of joints and improved posture many of the body's stresses can be relieved. This is a principle which was also used by an Australian actor, F M Alexander, in the late 19th century. Alexander found that his voice became strained during performances, and sometimes disappeared altogether. When studying himself in the mirror he found he restricted and tensed certain muscle groups, and tightened his throat muscles quite considerably. He taught himself to overcome this and went on to develop the technique which now bears his name, the Alexander Technique. This is popular with musicians and actors and the efficacy of the technique has been supported by research. Alexander believed that habitually poor posture influences the way the body and mind function, and that, when this happens, it is necessary to relearn basic movements. Alexander teachers educate students to become aware of patterns of misuse in everyday movements, paying particular attention to the way they hold their heads, and to align their body so that they are balanced and can move in a relaxed and fluid way. This technique changes individual habits of thought, feelings and movement by focusing on posture and body positioning. It teaches the individual how to use the right amount of effort in everyday activities, such as sitting, standing and walking, resulting in a reduction of stress previously caused by the body's imbalance.

Details of these and many other alternative therapies will be found in the Encyclopedia of Complementary Medicine[1] which has been written "to de-mystify the complexities and ambiguities of complementary medicine" and which will help you find the most effective and beneficial therapy for you. You will find addresses in the appendix, of organisations you can write to for lists of practitioners within your area. The very best way to find a good practitioner of any of the above treatments is to get a recommendation from someone else who is pleased with the treatment they have received, or classes they have attended. If you ask around amongst your friends and work colleagues you are sure to find people who are willing to talk about the treatments they have tried and the benefits, or otherwise, they have received. Your GP may also be able to recommend someone, although the advice you receive from an orthodox doctor may vary considerably. The medical profession has had a hard time believing in such treatments and the number of doctors keen to recommend them is still small, although attitudes are changing and there are practitioners of alternative medicine within some hospitals and GP's surgeries now. These developments are fuelled in modern times by the failure of drug-centred therapy to cure stress-related, environmental and psychological illness as well as long-term or recurring disease. Surgical accidents, negative side-effects of drugs, and a growing resistance to antibiotics have driven many doctors and medical researchers to look again at traditional folk medicine. A National Health Service practice to research complementary therapies has been established in the UK at the Marylebone Health Centre, London.

If you decide to consult an alternative therapist, choose someone who is properly qualified. They will take details of your medical history, and use treatment particularly designed for your condition. They will have adequate safeguards and abide by professional codes of practice. There are some conditions, pregnancy for example, which would not benefit and might even be harmed by some types of treatment, so always tell a practitioner of any medical condition you may have, and any medication you may be taking.

However, none of these disciplines will lessen the source of your stress. Whilst they may help your coping ability, their benefit will be in improving your physical well-being, perhaps by relieving tension or helping you to become more stress-proof. They will also complement good nutrition and exercise by helping you pay attention to the inner world of the emotions and spirit, and the way the interaction of these and other elements contributes to your general wellbeing. The health of the mind and body are inextricably interlinked. In helping you towards improved health of mind and body they will help you develop your inner resources and your energy in order to face the sources of your stress and take necessary action to reduce them.

Many of these therapies are useful in improving the quality of sleep and insomnia is one of the conditions which is found to greatly improve as a result of massage techniques, relaxation therapies and so on. The next chapter deals with the subject of insomnia and the mechanisms of sleep in more detail.

References

1. Woodham, Anne and Peters, David (1997) *Encyclopedia of Complementary Medicine*, Dorling Kindersley, London.

chapter fourteen

Can't sleep, won't sleep

Sleep is important to general health and wellbeing. Everybody needs sufficient sleep to enable them to perform their day's activities well and maintain their resistance to stress. If your job or your home circumstances are causing stress you need to ensure that you get adequate sleep. Ideally sleep should be taken all at once, but many people do very well on shorter naps during the day, and recent research supports the belief that people can catch up on lost sleep. The effects of stress can cause people to want to sleep more than is usual, but many people get by on very little sleep at all.

Jill

"Boom, boom." It sounded like distant gunfire. Jill turned over and thumped her pillow angrily. No, it wasn't the SAS on a dawn raid, but merely the advance guard, trundling wheelie bins to the edge of the kerb, in preparation for the wagon which would be along in an hour or two. "Why do they have to start at such an ungodly hour?" she asked of no one in particular. "I really needed my sleep this morning", she moaned, punctuating her lament with another thump on her pillow.

Wide awake now she turned over on to her back and spread herself across the width of the double bed, knowing that James had been up long since. He was probably already in his study reading through the huge pile of reports and documents which he brought home daily. He would have crept out of bed about six, started the day with some physical exercise, a shower and a light breakfast, and then have begun his day's reading, before driving to the office for about eight. He was chief executive of a large manufacturing company who only this year had taken over another one and were busy expanding and developing. It was a very exacting job and Jill marvelled at his ability to do this very demanding work after only five or six hours sleep per night. Not only that, he kept up this routine on holiday and had often been round the golf course before the rest of the family were up and about.

She herself still felt like a limp rag after even seven hours' sleep. It wasn't as if she didn't try. She got to bed early enough, that is so long as she didn't have extra work which kept her up late. She usually had a milky drink, because she'd heard this was a good soother at night. She always avoided coffee unless they'd been out for a meal when she couldn't resist the temptation of a cup, fresh brewed and aromatic.

She'd read in bed until she felt drowsy, trying to shut out the thoughts of all the things she had to do herself the next day, the appointments she had to keep, the meetings she had to attend, the staff problems she had to face. There never seemed to be enough time in the day to get through it all and she rushed from one task to the next, feeling like the White Rabbit in Alice in Wonderland, "I'm late, I'm late ...."

Last night had been pretty much the same as all the others. She'd eventually dozed off only to be woken what seemed like seconds later by the sound of their neighbours arriving back from a night out. Car doors slammed, garage doors rumbled, keys rattled and voices carried in the still night air. Jill silently fumed, "Really, some people have no consideration!" When all was silent again she turned over and composed herself for sleep once more, but now was aware of her full bladder and knew that she wouldn't get back to sleep until she'd visited the bathroom. Padding across the bedroom floor she could see the sleeping form of James, oblivious to it all, and uncharitable thoughts rose to mind.

Back in bed she'd eventually fallen asleep, where she'd found herself in the midst of a troubled dream, and woken with tears on her cheeks and feelings of great sadness, unable to fully recall the substance of the dream. Eventually she drifted off again, but here she was now, wide awake, no chance of getting back to sleep with the bin lorry about to make its noisy way down the road.

There was no point in going back to sleep, she had to be up in half an hour anyway. She reached for her dressing gown. "I know if I lie here fuming I'll start the day tense and probably develop a headache. I'd better look at this as positively as I can. It's extra time on the day, so I'll have an early breakfast and get in to work early myself. I'll be ahead of all the traffic and have some time in the office to myself to get on with a first draft of the presentation which I have to make to the board. I need to get this prepared by Wednesday anyway."

Winston Churchill is said never to have gone to bed during the whole of the Battle of Britain, but slept in a chair, snatching sleep when he could. Generally he got by on four or five hours per night. Margaret Thatcher is also said to have run the country on a similar amount of sleep. They are examples of people who needed very little sleep whilst doing a very demanding job.

We also begin to notice that as we get older our bodies need less sleep, and if you aren't sleeping for the same length of time as you used to it may be because you no longer need as much. After all a baby (if you are lucky) sleeps nearly 24 hours a day when it is first born, and one of the signs of increasing maturity in an infant is the fact that it needs less and less sleep. As we get older this pattern is not as marked but is still noticeable. What is important is that we get regular sleep and recognise our own individual need.

Thomas Edison invented the light bulb so that people would not have to waste the hours of darkness in sleep. This means that we can now carry on both our work and our leisure activities into the hours of darkness. But it also means that we have become less aware of our body's natural rhythms and can neglect our need for sleep. It is natural for human beings to want to sleep during the night and wake up during the day time, regulated by a biological clock. This clock is located in the hypothalamus, deep in the brain. This also triggers the desire to sleep longer in the winter and rise earlier during the summer, so it is not just that you wish you could hibernate until the warmer weather arrives. It seems your body is designed to prompt you to do that.

This biological clock is known as the circadian rhythm[1]. As well as being responsible for our waking and sleeping cycle, it controls our body temperature, and our hormones, triggering melatonin, the natural sleep hormone. Practitioners of Ayurvedic medicine[2], who pay attention to these natural rhythms, advise us that the natural bedtime occurs around 10 pm. If we postpone going to sleep much beyond this point we miss the rejuvenating effect that begins at the start of the next cycle. It seems that there might be some truth in what our mothers always told us, that an hour before midnight is worth two after. The brain's lowest ebb, the body's lowest temperature and our lowest blood glucose levels all occur before dawn. Which is why, when we are awake in the night, our worries and fears take on exaggerated importance which diminishes with the onset of daylight.

In order to combat stress, pay attention to your body's need for sleep and develop a good sleep pattern. A normal sleep pattern goes something like this. To begin with you feel drowsy, your mind wanders and you often drift in and out of sleep without being aware of it. If you are disturbed at this time you will swear that you have not yet been to sleep, and in fact the slightest noise or touch will bring you wide awake again. Many people find that good ideas come to them at this time, between sleep and wakefulness. I often find myself solving crossword puzzle clues, or coming up with a good idea for a training programme. This is known as ideational activity.

Within half an hour it is likely that you will be fully asleep, and an hour later will have reached a deeper stage of sleep. Within another hour you go into an even deeper stage of REM (rapid eye movement) sleep lasting about 15 minutes and it is during this stage you are likely to dream. Then the cycle occurs again shallow, deeper, deepest - throughout the night. I have been known to sleep in the same room as a ringing telephone and be totally unaware of it, but at other times I have come wide awake at a the drip of a tap from the bathroom. It depends on which part of the sleep cycle you are in. It is in this phase of REM sleep when the important recharging and repairing of our body and mind take place, and the dreaming which occurs is an important safety valve. People who are deprived of REM sleep are likely to suffer from depression, fatigue, restlessness, irritability, anger and depression.

Our sleep cycle is a significant source of energy and if we have developed a natural rhythm so that we wake at our natural point we can be quick, alert, enthusiastic and exhilarated. If we miss our natural waking point when we are rudely awakened by the clanging alarm, or have a lie-in, we miss the phase and can wake up dull, heavy and slow. If this becomes habitual our whole physiology can become sluggish in response.

To develop better resistance to stress and beat insomnia, try to find out how much sleep your body really needs. How much sleep a night do you get on average? If you spend eight hours in bed but are only asleep for four or five you may not need eight hours of sleep. In order to get your body into the habit of making full use of those five hours, and to get REM sleep, try going to bed later and set the alarm to wake you up after five hours. If you sleep throughout the four to five hours you can then go to bed half an hour earlier the following night and set the alarm for five and a half hours Keep doing this until your body is getting all its sleep at one time, and the amount of sleep you are having seems to be what your body needs.

But a word about alarm clocks. Being jolted out of deep sleep by the sound of a loud bell or buzzer is not the most pleasant experience and is likely to leave you feeling irritable and out of sorts for most of the day. Try a radio alarm which brings you gently awake, or better still try to set your body's natural alarm. One of my colleagues does this by saying to her subconscious, just before she goes to sleep, "I will wake up at ...." and she gives it a time a few minutes before the time at which she has set the alarm. She finds it very effective, and is thinking of dispensing with her alarm altogether.

If you are someone who finds your body does not want a lot of sleep, think of this positively and be grateful. This is a gift of extra time added to your life, use it. Do not waste it lying in bed wishing you were asleep, pretending to be asleep, or berating yourself for not falling asleep. No one ever died through lack of sleep. Given the opportunity, your body will take the rest that it needs. It's not the lack of sleep which causes problems, it is our mental state. If you worry about not sleeping, the worry makes the insomnia worse, making it harder to get off to sleep, and causing you to feel like a chewed rag next day. You will feel much better if you spend the night relaxing, even if you have not slept much.

Usually people do get a necessary amount of sleep but stay in the first light stages of sleep which can often feel like being awake. Your partner may assure you that you have been snoring all night. When you are worrying or your mind is still active, you are producing adrenaline. When this is happening it cannot produce melatonin which you need to help you get off to sleep. This is why it is so difficult to get off to sleep if you have been working late, or enjoying yourself and your mind is still active as you try to drop off. At these times you may find that doing a relaxation exercise before you go to bed will help. This will help to switch off the adrenaline. Reading, solving crossword puzzles, listening to music or meditation tapes can also help. One of my colleagues in the Health Service, as part of her job, had to regularly survey a lot of rather dull literature. She told me she saved it up to read at bedtime and bored herself to sleep!

So worrying is counterproductive. When you lie awake, or are up in the middle of the night, try to be positive and say to yourself, "I will try to see the fact that I am awake not as a problem, but as an opportunity. I will keep myself relaxed and try to go back to sleep again later."

During my life, particularly as I have reached the menopause, I find myself having difficulty sleeping through the night. Once it was just difficulty getting off to sleep, as my mind was replaying all the events of the day and planning all the things I had to do the next day. Later it was waking up at three or four in the morning and finding myself wide awake, completely unable to go back to sleep.

Over time I have developed ways of keeping myself sane, and enabling myself to carry on with my daily life in spite of very little sleep some nights. One of my favourites, apart from deep breathing and relaxing, is to keep my least favourite job, in my case the ironing, on hand, to do in the night. When I have been awake for a while I say to myself, "Does it seem like I'm not going to get back to sleep? Shall I get up and do the ironing?" Quite often my mind says, "No!" and I turn over and quickly go back to sleep. If I wake in the early morning and it is daylight, I am usually quite glad to get up, and much of the first part of this book was written between four and eight in the morning.

Consider the common impediments to rest. Many people are unable to sleep because they are over-stimulated, often by things they have ingested earlier in the day such as caffeine, cold remedies, herbal products. Others cannot sleep because of noise or aches and pains. Some cannot switch off their minds. There are simple remedies for all of these problems.

First of all remember that you only sleep when you are tired, so get up earlier in the morning, or go to bed later at night. Try to take more exercise during the day and walk instead of using the car (that will be good for the environment too). But remember to allow a couple of hours winding down after exercise before going to bed. Try to prevent yourself from cat napping during the day, but use the Power Nap to re-energise yourself.

Empty your bladder before you go to bed and try not having anything to drink later in the evening. Make sure that any drinks you do have do not contain caffeine. Caffeine is a diuretic (that means it makes you produce more urine). Some alcoholic drinks, gin for instance, are also diuretics.

Comfort is important. Are you warm enough? Use an electric blanket or hot water bottle if you need to. Check your mattress and your pillows. It may be time to buy new ones, or even to try a new type such as a water bed or a futon. Use natural fibres for sheets, blankets, duvets and night clothes as they allow your body to breathe and absorb perspiration. You might also try a herb pillow, or a few drops of an appropriate aromatherapy oil (lavender for example) on your pillow. Consider ventilation in your bedroom too: have you enough, or too much?

Your bedroom should be an environment in which you feel relaxed. Make sure your decor is pleasing and has a soothing influence. Watching TV or working in the bedroom can be too stimulating and destroy the relaxing ambience. Resist the temptation to set up your sewing machine, or computer in there. This can be bad for your love life too. Making your bedroom more soundproof can be another way of making it more relaxing and comfortable. Heavy curtains, double glazing, thick pile carpet, all help to absorb the noise. If you have noisy neighbours on the other side of a party wall could you cover that wall with a fitted wardrobe or thick, full-length curtains to absorb the sound, or move into another room?

Cotton wool in your ears, or specially designed foam ear plugs bought from the chemist, can also help, as can the kind of masks which they give you on an aeroplane, to block out the light. You might also consider buying a white noise generator. This is an electronic device that produces restful sound. White noise contains a mixture of many different frequencies of sound waves, just as white light contains all frequencies of visible light. It sounds like water running from a shower head, and most units have variable controls that allow you to change the basic sound from that of a steady downpour to rhythmic ocean waves. White noise is soothing and masks offending sounds, so it is particularly valuable for tinnitus sufferers.

If you are being kept awake by physical problems such as pain, cramps, difficulty in breathing or similar problems, make sure that you are comfortable and warm. Use deep breathing exercises, to increase your pain threshold. But do try to treat the cause of the pain, if you know what it is, and if it persists ask your doctor's advice. You might also consult an osteopath or a chiropractor who will help correct any bone misalignments which might be causing pain or discomfort. If you have a partner you could encourage him or her to give you a massage before bedtime which could be a very pleasing way to end the day for both of you.

Exercise, fresh air, and natural light during waking hours are all important factors in sleep regulation. People who work in air-conditioned offices with poor natural lighting often find it hard to sleep. Lack of sunlight is thought to slow down the production of melatonin, and whilst we are discouraged from spending hours basking in the hot sun because of the dangers of ultra-violet light, do not deny yourself some gentle sunlight. This is vital to health and well-being, and essential to the insomniac. Office air-conditioning can also remove as much as one litre of water from the body in just a few hours so drink plenty to replace it.

Digestive processes can interfere with sleep because it requires an increase in metabolism which can cause you to be wakeful. Do not eat a meal too late before going to bed, nor go to bed hungry. Avoid greasy, salty and heavy foods. Try a milky drink and a couple of biscuits before going to bed, and make sure that your evening meal is high in carbohydrate and low in protein. Coffee, tea and alcohol are stimulants.

It is particularly important that you should use your relaxation skills to help you get off to sleep. Some people find a warm (not hot) bath is relaxing, particularly if it contains a herbal muscle relaxant. Do avoid the use of sleeping pills or tranquillisers, particularly those of the benzodiazepine type. These are only useful in the short term as their effect gradually wears off, you find you need to keep increasing your dose to get the same effect, and they may affect your functioning during the day. Even after using them for a short time they will interrupt your normal sleep pattern by suppressing REM sleep, and the insomnia can be worse when you stop taking them. If you are already on this type of medication do not stop suddenly, or severe withdrawal symptoms which mimic your original problem, only worse, are likely to occur. Reduce your dose very, very gradually and get some help from one of the self-help groups for tranquilliser users.

Andrew Weil[3] recommends valerian as a safe sedative. He describes this as a natural remedy obtained from the root of a European plant, Valerian officinalis. It can be bought in health food stores and drunk as a tea. But valerian is a depressant and that too should not be used for more than a brief time.

He also mentions a non-addictive, non-depressant regulator of sleep cycles which has become available in the USA, melatonin, the hormone secreted by the pineal gland, which regulates the biological clock. International travellers who are able to buy this in the States say that it is the first really effective treatment for jet lag, especially for west-to-east travel, (which most people find harder). It appears safe and effective for resetting biological clocks. It sounds wonderful and a desperate insomniac may wish to try it. For myself I remember the introduction of tranquillisers in the sixties when they were hailed as safe and non-addictive. Later research has discovered that they are a scourge, from which it is nearly impossible to withdraw, and that users become chemically addicted. So I can understand why melotonin is still not available in the UK.

One of the greatest sources of mental turmoil today is the daily news in papers and TV broadcasts which focus more and more on bad news. You have a choice of whether you let this information into your mind and thoughts. If the news keeps you awake, choose not to listen just before going to bed.

When all else fails and you find yourself awake in the night, and if you really know you are not going to get off to sleep, think about getting up and making use of the extra time you have. You can, like myself, get up to do something you want to do and for which you do not usually get the time. It can be a useful time for study or starting that book you keep promising to read. My early morning world is always shared by a handful of dedicated golfers on the course that I can see from my study window. Perhaps they are insomniacs too. So, insomnia is not the end of the world. There are many things you can do to help you get a good night's sleep, and many ways to use the extra time that less sleep gives you. Above all do not worry about not sleeping and you will still be refreshed and able to go about your daily work. Your body will make up the lost sleep some other time, if you give it the opportunity.

References

1. Marsden, Kathryn (1995) *All Day Energy*, Bantam Books, Cox and Wyman, Reading.

2. Chopra, Deepak (1995) *Boundless Energy*, Random House, UK.

3. Weil, Andrew (1995) *Spontaneous Healing*, Warner Books, London.

chapter fifteen

Handling stress effectively prolongs active life

I hope that by this stage you are beginning to realise that there is a lot you can do to help yourself to handle the stress in your life in such a way that you can continue to get the most out of your life, and work towards the achievement of all your long-term goals.

Look first of all at your lifestyle. Are you as healthy as you might be with sensible eating, and drinking habits? Are you as fit as you could be and is your weight what it should be for a person of your height? Do you avoid the use of drugs including nicotine, and do you maintain your caffeine, alcohol and sugar intake at sensible levels? How much sleep are you getting and does it seem like refreshing sleep, or do you wake up tired? Do you take regular breaks, have at least one absorbing hobby and socialise with people from outside your own professional group or work area?

The way in which you have answered these questions will give you an indication of how stress-proof you are likely to be and setting yourself targets for improvement in some of these areas may be the first step you need to take in order to help you to be less susceptible to the effects of stress.

Having ensured that you have done all that you can to prepare yourself for the waves of stress the next area to consider is what you can do to prevent stress. Have you listed your sources of stress and made sensible, rational decisions about what you might be able to do to prevent some of that stress? Have you decided which things you can change, and which things you will need to learn to accept? How can you pilot your own life?

Are you able to use good time-management skills, and have you the confidence to communicate clearly and assertively when you choose to do so? This includes the ability to say "No" to things that are not your responsibility, without feeling guilty.

Other stresses cannot be prevented. The choice you are faced with then is either coping with them, or avoiding them. How necessary is this stressor in your life? If it cannot be avoided, the techniques you need to practice are those of keeping yourself from being overwhelmed by the stressor, and handling the stress to the very best of your ability. If it is something which is not a necessary part of your life, or the stress that it is causing is greater than you wish to cope with, then you may think of avoiding it or getting away from it completely. If you cannot avoid it and choose to live with it, develop your coping skills. If you cannot avoid it and choose to live with it, develop your coping skills. You can change your thoughts, and when you change your thoughts you will find that your emotions change too. Acknowledging the emotions is also very useful, once they come to the surface you can do something about them.

Don't forget also to have good techniques for bouncing back when the waves of stress have passed.

Practise the breathing exercises and use the body check and relaxation exercises daily in order to reduce the tension and renew your energy.

There are many people out there only too willing to help you, and outside help may be what you need if your own amount of adaptation energy is becoming depleted. Remember to make the most of these resources. Who could you talk to in the first instance? Do you have a sympathetic employer, family member, or friend? What form of alternative help would benefit you most? If stress is affecting you psychologically perhaps a counsellor a hypnotherapist is what you need, or you could learn deep meditation or relaxation techniques. If stress is affecting you physically have a medical check up and consider one of the more physical forms of alternative therapy, Shiatsu or massage, perhaps.

It is whilst you are coping with the stress that you need to be ever alert to how you are perceiving the stressor, remembering that if you allow yourself to get overstressed before doing something about it, you may have difficulty working out a rational solution. This will not be a problem if you remember to take the breaks you are entitled to and always have a lunch hour so that you return to your work refreshed. If you bear in mind the 80:20 principle you can start by tackling the 20% of daily hassles that are really stressing you out.

Whatever you decide that you need to do, remember that the remedy is in your hands. No one need be a victim. One person's stress is another person's challenge, and at the end of the day it comes down to perceptions. You may be unemployed and viewing your friends who are in work with envy. They, in turn, might be putting in long hours at a stressful job and longing for the day when they can retire and have the time at home that you have.

Maintain your sense of humour and practice positive thinking, as well as taking regular exercise and finding ways of releasing the tension. After stressful events or periods of high tension use your relaxation and breathing techniques to help you regain your equilibrium. Take a break, use your holiday entitlement, and choose some of the Small Delights to reward yourself for your hard work.

We all view things differently and have choices only we can make, and I hope that reading this book has helped you to make the necessary choices for your life, and to maintain your energy levels in the healthy challenge section of the performance-pressure curve. In so doing you will be taking action which will help you remain healthy and increase the likelihood of a long and active retirement.

1. Are you type A or type B personality?

My typical behaviour	Never	Sometimes	Usually	Always
I get irritated when things don't go the way I want them to, or the way I plan them.	1	2	3	4
I am restless and get frustrated when I have to stand in queues, or wait in traffic jams (e.g. I change queues in supermarkets).	1	2	3	4
Other people seem to me to be selfish or stubborn	1	2	3	4
I feel that people who get in my way are pushy or thoughtless and I become hostile	1	2	3	4
I find myself completing other people's sentences, or "putting words in their mouths" to hurry things along	1	2	3	4
My actions are quick and my speech is rushed	1	2	3	4
I am very competitive, and measure myself and my performance against other people	1	2	3	4
I have intense drive and ambition	1	2	3	4
My self-esteem depends on what I can achieve	1	2	3	4
I find it hard to leave work at the end of the day	1	2	3	4
I often push myself when I feel tired	1	2	3	4
I often leave jobs to the last minute then panic	1	2	3	4
I often allow insufficient time to get to work or important appointments	1	2	3	4
I often try to do two or more things at once	1	2	3	4
I often eat whilst I am working	1	2	3	4
Total				

The higher the score the greater your pre-disposition towards stress.

Scores above 40 reflect a so-called "Type A" behaviour pattern, showing an overdeveloped sense of time urgency, and competitiveness. This behaviour may have short-term benefits, but in the long run may increase the risk of illness. Scores can be reduced by slowing down, paying attention to the humour and beauty in life, focusing more on the quality of your relationships. If you consistently rush and compete you will experience frustration which makes physical and emotional demands on the cardiovascular system. This is only a problem when it is unconscious and automatic. Hurrying and competitiveness are not a health risk when there is a specific reason, because they do not constantly drain your energy.

Remember you cannot change your personality, but you can change the way you behave.

2. Life change index

In 1973 T H Holmes and R H Rae developed this index so that the possibility of health change in people could be measured. By looking at the number and type of changes which had occurred during the previous twelve months it was possible to predict the chance of any individual experience a major change in their health. This Index takes no account of age, race, education, class or that some people have more adaptation energy than others. Remember it is not what happens to you that is the problem, it is what you do with what happens to you. Also whether an event is a source of stress to you depends on how you view it

Read through the list and tick the changes you have experienced in the last twelve months. Then total up the points and compare your score with those outlined below.

Death of partner	100	Responsibility change	29
Divorce	73	Child leaves home	29
Separation from partner	65	In-law problems	29
Jail sentence	63	Partner starts or stops work	26
Death of close family member	63	Starting a new school	26
Personal illness or injury	53	Leaving school	26
Marriage	50	Changes in living conditions	25
Loss of job	47	Changes in personal habits	24
Reconciliation with marriage partner	45	Trouble with employer	23
Retirement	45	Change in work hours	20
Health problem of close family member	44	Moving house	20
Pregnancy	40	Change in recreation	19
Sex problems	39	Change in religious activities	18
Addition to family	39	Small mortgage or loan	17
Major changes at work	39	Change in sleeping habits	16
Changes in financial position	39	Changes in number/type of family gatherings	15
Death of friend	37	Major change in eating pattern	15
Changes of work	36	Holiday	13
Changes in number of arguments with partner	35	Christmas	12
Mortgage or loan foreclosed	30	Minor violations of law	11

150-199 points increases your likelihood of illness by 40%
200-299 points increases your likelihood of illness by 50%
300 points and over increases your likelihood of illness by 80%

Reference: Holmes and Rahe, 'Scaling of Life Change' in the *Journal of Psychosomatic Research*, June, 1967

3. Managing stress questionnaire

Coping checklist

The following checklist is designed to provide a very rough and superficial approximation of how well you are now coping with your job. It is adapted from the checklist in "Work Stress" by AA McClean (1979), Addison Wesley.

To what extent does each of the following fit as a description of you? (Circle one number on each line across).

	Very true	Quite true	Somewhat true	Not very true	Not at all true
1. I "roll with the punches" when problems come up	1	2	3	4	5
2. I spend almost all my time thinking about my work	5	4	3	2	1
3. I treat other people as individuals and care about their feelings and opinions	1	2	3	4	5
4. I recognise and accept my own limitations and assets	1	2	3	4	5
5. There are quite a few people I could describe as 'good friends'	1	2	3	4	5
6. I enjoy using my skills and abilities on and off the job	1	2	3	4	5
7. I get bored easily	5	4	3	2	1
8. I enjoy meeting and talking with people who have different ways of thinking about the world	1	2	3	4	5
9. Often in my job I 'bite off more than I can chew'	5	4	3	2	1
10. I'm usually very active at weekends with projects or recreation	1	2	3	4	5
11. I prefer working with people who are very much like myself	5	4	3	2	1
12. I work mainly because I have to live and not necessarily because I enjoy what I do	5	4	3	2	1
13. I believe I have a realistic picture of my personal strengths and weaknesses	1	2	3	4	5
14. I often get into arguments with people who don't think my way	5	4	3	2	1
15. I often have trouble getting much done on my job	5	4	3	2	1
16. I'm interested in a lot of different topics	1	2	3	4	5

	Very true	Quite true	Some-what true	Not very true	Not at all true
17. I get upset when things don't go my way	5	4	3	2	1
18. Often, I'm not sure where I stand on a controversial topic	5	4	3	2	1
19. I'm usually able to find a way round anything which stops me from an important goal	1	2	3	4	5
20. I often disagree with my boss or others at work	5	4	3	2	1

For scoring directions see appendix 6

4. Managing stress questionnaire

Context survey

How do you feel about each of the following in your job? (Circle one number in each line across)

	Very satis-fied	Satis-fied	Neut-ral	Dis-satis-fied	Very satis-fied
1. How satisfied are you with the company you work for compared with other companies you know about?	1	2	3	4	5
2. How satisfied are you with your job - the kind of work you do?	1	2	3	4	5
3. How satisfied are you with your physical working conditions (heat, light, noise etc.)	1	2	3	4	5
4. How satisfied are you with the extent to which people you work with co-operate well with one another?	1	2	3	4	5
5. How satisfied are you with the job your immediate supervisor is doing in managing his or her responsibilities for people?	1	2	3	4	5
6. How satisfied are you with the job your immediate supervisor is doing in managing his or her task or functional responsibilities?	1	2	3	4	5
7. How satisfied are you with your pay, considering your duties and responsibilities?	1	2	3	4	5
8. How satisfied are you with your pay considering what other companies pay for similar types of work?	1	2	3	4	5
9. How satisfied are you with your advancement to better jobs since you started to work with your company?	1	2	3	4	5
10. How satisfied are you with your opportunities to move into a better job in the company?	1	2	3	4	5
11. How satisfied are you with the extent to which your present job makes full use of your skills and abilities?	1	2	3	4	5

	Very satis- fied	Satis- fied	Neut- ral	Dis- satis- fied	Very satis- fied
12. How satisfied are you with the level of mental ability requirements of your present job (problem solving, judgement, technical knowledge etc.)?	1	2	3	4	5
13. How satisfied are you with the level of average time demands of your present job (hours worked, as opposed to mental ability demands)?	1	2	3	4	5
14. Now considering everything how would you rate your overall feelings about your employment situation at the present time?	1	2	3	4	5

15. If you have your way, will you be working for your present organisation five years from now? Circle one:

1. Certainly   4. Probably not
2. Probably   5. Certainly not
3. I'm not at all sure   6. I'll be retired in five years

For scoring directions see appendix 6

5. Managing stress questionnaire

Stressors checklist

Listed below are various kinds of problems that may - or may not - arise in your work. Indicate to what extent you find each of them to be a problem, concern or obstacle in carrying out your job duties and responsibilities. (This checklist obviously does not include possible off-the-job sources of stress.)

	Never	Sel-dom	Some-times	Usu-ally	Always
Conflict and uncertainty					
1. Not knowing just what the people you work with expect of you	1	2	3	4	5
2. Feeling that you have to do things on the job that are against your better judgement	1	2	3	4	5
3. Thinking that you will not be able to satisfy the conflicting demands of various people over you	1	2	3	4	5
Job pressure					
4. Feeling that you have too heavy a workload; one that you can't possibly finish during an ordinary day	1	2	3	4	5
5. Not having enough time to do the work properly	1	2	3	4	5
6. Having the requirements of the job conflict with/impose upon your personal life	1	2	3	4	5
Job scope					
7. Being unclear about just what the scope and responsibilities of your job are	1	2	3	4	5
8. Feeling that you have too little authority to carry out the responsibilities assigned to you	1	2	3	4	5
9. Not being able to get the information you need to carry out your job	1	2	3	4	5

	Never	Sel- dom	Some- times	Usu- ally	Always
Rapport with management					
10. Not knowing what your manager or supervisor thinks of you - how he or she evaluates your performance	1	2	3	4	5
11. Not being able to predict the reactions of people above you	1	2	3	4	5
12. Having ideas considerably different from those of your managers	1	2	3	4	5

For scoring see appendix 6

6. Managing stress questionnaire

Scoring directions

Appendix 3 - Coping checklist

Add together the numbers you circled for the four questions in each of the coping scales (see below for the appropriate questions).

Coping scale	Add together the answers to these questions	Your score (write in)
Knows self	4, 9, 13, 18	_____
Many interests	2, 5, 7, 16	_____
Variety of reactions	1, 11, 17, 19	_____
Accepts other values	3, 8, 14, 20	_____
Active and productive	6, 10, 12, 15	_____

Add the five scores together for the total score

Scores for each area can vary between 5 and 20.

Scores of 12 or more suggest it may be useful to direct more attention to that area.

The overall score can range between 20 and 100.

Scores of 60 or more may suggest some general difficulty in coping with the areas covered.

Appendix 4 - Context checklist

Add together the numbers you circled and enter the total here _____

Scores on this survey range between 14 and 75.

Scores of 45 or more suggest the overall context of your work is less than satisfactory.

You should also look at the specific items you rated negatively.

Appendix 5 - Stressors checklist

Add together the three numbers you circled within each of the four areas and enter them here:

Conflict and uncertainty _____

Job pressure _____

Job scope _____

Rapport with management _____

The add them all together for total score _____

Scores on each of the four areas can range between 3 and 15.

Scores of 9 and above may suggest that the area may be presenting a problem which warrants your attention.

The overall total score can range between 12 and 60. Scores of 36 or more may suggest a more than desirable amount of stress in your job environment.

7. Reactions to change

Think about the changes happening at work. Circle the number in the column that corresponds to your reaction.

	Never	Some times	Us-ually ways	Al-
Changes happen too quickly	1	2	3	4
I look forward to change	1	2	3	4
Whenever there's a change I look for the opportunities	1	2	3	4
My manager asks for my opinions about change	1	2	3	4
I try things out even if they don't work out in the end	1	2	3	4
I worry about having to learn new things	1	2	3	4
There are too many changes happening	1	2	3	4
Change leads to improvements	1	2	3	4
It's up to the managers to implement the changes	1	2	3	4
I prefer to do things the same way	1	2	3	4
I am well informed about changes by my manager	1	2	3	4
I find coping with change as well as my workload, very tiring	1	2	3	4
For me, change is more negative than positive	1	2	3	4
I'm asked for suggestions about changes	1	2	3	4
Most people change things for the sake of change	1	2	3	4

Total

Add up the numbers you circled. The higher your score, the more resistant you are likely to be to change. If you scored more than 30, you should ask yourself if this is because of

a) your attitude?

b) the nature of the change? or

c) the way the change is being managed?

Based on "A Change For The Better" in *Changing People*, video-based training material produced and distributed by Seven Dimensions Pty Ltd, 18 Armstrong Street Middle Park, Victoria, Australia 3206.

Useful addresses

Acupressure and acupuncture

The British Medical Acupuncture Society
Newton House
Newton Lane
Whitley
Warrington
Cheshire. WA4 4JA
Tel: 01925 730727
For information about acupuncturists who are also medical doctors.

British Acupuncture Council
Park House
206-208 Latimer Road
London. W10 6RE
Free list of local therapists available, or send £3.50 for complete register

Alexander technique

The Society of Teachers of the Alexander Technique
20 London House
266 Fulham Road
London. SW10 9EL
Tel: 0171 351 0828

Aromatherapy

Aromatherapy Organisations Council
3 Latymer Close
Braybrooke
Market Harborough
Leicester. LE16 8LN
Tel/Fax: 01858 434242
Send A5 SAE to the secretary for information

Chiropractic

The British Chiropractic Association
Equity House
29 Whitley Street
Reading
Berkshire. RG2 0EG
Send £5.75 for register.

The McTimoney Chiropractic Association
21 High Street
Eynsham
Oxfordshire. OX8 1HE
Send £2 cheque for information pack.

Counselling

British Association for Counselling (BAC)
Regent Place
Rugby
Warwickshire. CV21 2PJ
Their resources directory, also available from local libraries, gives updated list of national organisations, local centres and individual counsellors and therapists, with their special interests. There are useful tips on finding the right kind of help.

Cruse (Bereavement counselling)
Cruse House
126 Sheen Road
Richmond
Surrey. TW9 1UR

Relate (Couples' counselling)
Herbert Gray College
Little Church Street
Rugby
Warwickshire. CV21 3AP

Flotation

Float Tank Association UK
PO Box 11024,
London. SW4 7ZF
Tel: 0171 627 4962

Hypnotherapy

The National Register of Hypnotherapists & Psychotherapists
12 Cross Street
Nelson
Lancashire.BB9 7EN
Tel: 01282 699378
send SAE

Osteopathy

The General Council & Register of Osteopaths
PO Box 2074
Reading
Berkshire. RG1 4YR
Tel: 0118 951 2051
Send SAE

Reflexology

The Association of Reflexologists
27 Old Gloucester Street
London. WC1N 3XX
Tel: 0990 673320
send A4 SAE for free copy of register.

Relaxation

The Relaxation for Living Trust
Foxhills
30 Victoria Avenue
Shanklin
Isle of Wight. PO37 6LS

Shiatsu

The Shiatsu Society
Interchange Studios
Dalby St.
London. NW5 3NQ
Tel: 0171 813 7772
Send SAE for information

Transcendental meditation

The Transcendental Meditation Association
FREEPOST
London SW1P 4YY
Tel: 0990 143733
Books and tapes are available.

Yoga

The British Wheel of Yoga
1 Hamilton Place
Boston Road
Sleaford
Lincolnshire. NG34 7ES
Tel: 01529 306851

Other useful addresses

Complementary medicine

The Institute for Complementary
Medicine (ICM)
PO Box 194
London. SE16 1QZ
Send SAE and two loose first class stamps for
list of practitioners.

Homeopathy

The UK Homeopathic Medical Association
6 Livingstone Road
Gravesend
Kent. DA12 5DZ
Telephone: 01474 560336

Society of Homeopaths
2 Artisan Road
Northampton. NN1 4HU
Tel: 01604 21400
Send a large SAE.

Health education

The Health Education Authority
Hamilton House
Mabeldon Place
London. WC1H 9TX
Tel: 0171 383 3833
For information about diet, alcohol, caffeine,
smoking, drugs and general health care.
Central telephone number for the nearest
Health Information Centre.
Tel: 0800 665544

Stress

The International Stress Management
Association (UK Branch)
Division of Psychology
South Bank University
103 Borough Road
London SE1 0AA
List of members from a wide range of
disciplines and specialities who have extra, or
special, expertise in stress management.

Tranquilliser Addiction
CITA (Counselling for Involuntary
Tranquilliser Addiction)
Cavendish House
Brighton Road
Waterloo
Liverpool. L22 5NG
Helpline: 0151 949 0102
10am - 1pm Mon to Fri

Further reading

Warren, Eve, and Toll, Caroline (1993) *The Stress Work Book*, Nicholas Brealey, London.

Black, Ken and Kate (1982) *Assertiveness at Work*, McGraw Hill, London.

Blanchard, Kenneth, and Johnson, Spencer, *The One Minute Manager*, Willow Books.

Block, Peter (1990) *The Empowered Manager: Positive Political Skills at Work*, Jossey-Bass Inc.

Cooper, Cary L. and Williams Stephen (1994) *Creating Healthy Work Organisations*, John Wiley and Sons.

Glouberman, Dina (1989) *Life Choices and Life Changes Through Imagework: The Art of Developing Personal Vision*, Harper Collins.

Goliszek, Dr. Andrew (1993) *60 Second Stress Management*, Cox andman Ltd., Reading.

Jeffers Susan (1998) *Feel the Fear and Beyond*, Random House UK Ltd.

Knight, Sue (1995) *NLP at Work*, Nicholas Brealey Publishing, London.

Robbins, Anthony (1991) *Notes From A Friend*, Simon and Schuster.